Pioneers of the Soul

Pioneers of the Soul

The Last Teachings of
Hilda Charlton

Golden Quest
Woodstock, New York

Pioneers of the Soul
The Last Teachings of Hilda Charlton

Published by:
GOLDEN QUEST
P.O. Box 190
Lake Hill, New York 12448

Authorized by the International Publications Council of Golden Quest

First Edition

Printed in the United States of America

ISBN 0-927383-12-8

Table of Contents

About Hilda Charlton

Hilda Charlton was a spiritual teacher, author, dancer and healer who touched and uplifted the lives of many thousands during the twenty-three years that she taught classes in meditation and prayer in New York City.

Born in London, Hilda moved to the United States with her parents when she was four years old. She was raised in Salt Lake City, Utah, and Los Angeles, California. At the age of eighteen she began performing as a modern dancer, and for the next two decades she danced and taught in the San Francisco area. From 1947 to 1950, Hilda toured India and Ceylon as a dancer. She stayed in India and Ceylon for fifteen more years, pursuing her studies of Eastern mysticism and meditation. She was guided by great spiritual masters and holy people, including Sri Nityananda of Ganeshpuri, Sri Mahadevananda of Bombay, and Sri Sathya Sai Baba of Puttaparthi.

Upon her return to America, Hilda settled in New York City. She was asked to teach by those she met, and over the years her classes grew in size from two people to more than a thousand. The location was moved from a student's apartment to the basement of St. Luke's Church, and in 1976 to the nave and later to the Synod House of the Cathedral Church of St. John the Divine.

Her teachings incorporated the fundamental principles of the world's major religions. Foremost in her classes she stressed the importance of a life of giving and forgiving, unconditional love and remembrance of God.

Hilda's lectures included poignant stories of her life, practical lessons for everyday living, and guidance in prayer and meditation. Her style combined humor, practicality and deep insight into the human mind and spirit.

Her teachings had a profound effect on the lives of thousands of people from all walks of life. Alcoholics and drug addicts were known to conquer their addictions, prostitutes left the streets, and those afflicted with serious diseases often reported experiencing remission and cure.

She passed on in New York City on January 29, 1988.

Hilda Charlton

Introduction

*We are entering a new life — a new way of thinking, a new
way of acting, a complete turnabout. We are walking on virgin
soil which has never been trod on this Earth. We are pioneers of
the soul, leading humanity back to God.*

Hilda

God has a magnificent plan in store for humanity: the Golden Age of God,
a time of love, harmony and balance is soon to dawn upon this Earth. But
first the old has to die inwardly and outwardly: the personality must
undergo a time of tribulation to learn the way of unconditional love; and
the outer forms of life that reflect the old way of selfishness and fear must
undergo dissolution. The old mentality is destroying our world with crass
disregard for the integrity of our environment and is bringing our planet
dangerously close to self-annihilation.

We live in a time of both dire crisis and great possibility, for even as the
old is dying, the energies initiating a new life on Earth are emerging. In her
last year, knowing that she would not be much longer on Earth, Hilda
emphasized the coming of the crisis to impress deeply on her "kids" the
urgency of fundamental personal change. She was a master of the Earth
school, and she believed in the innate wisdom, power and love in each and
every person. She worked with all her strength to bring forth in people this
inner reality, for that alone is humanity's solution to the distress it has
brought on itself. Those who take refuge in the divinity within, she stressed,
will be able to withstand the adversity of these times; indeed, if enough
people would only turn to God and undertake personal transformation,
then the most dire consequences of humanity's greed and selfishness could
be averted.

Choose the life regenerate, she urged, and you will find not distress but rather increasing light and joy.

This is our sacred charge from Hilda: to be pioneers of the soul, builders of the New Age of God. It is a charge we cannot ignore, for humanity's very unfoldment hangs in the balance.

Chapter One

Reborn in the Holy Spirit

I come tonight to bring you glad tidings.[1] These times we now live in on planet Earth will pass away, and we shall see the glory of God's plan for all — a time of peace and plenty. Mother Earth is now in her ninth month, and soon the New Age of God will be born and Mother Earth will get spiritualized.

These are exciting, exhilarating times, wonderful times, for they harbor the coming of the Kingdom of God, the age of truth and glory. Yet they are terrifying times for those who have no faith or trust in God and in the Christ who dwells within.

The highest creatures on Earth are woman and man. It is our duty and task to carry out the completion of the spiritualization of the Earth. That's all you're here for, nothing else, not to do all those great things you are doing, but to spiritualize the Earth wherever you are. If you're a school-teacher, then see that you stay spiritual all day. If you work in the home or out in the world earning a living, wherever you are, you spiritualize that part of the Earth and your body in preparation. That is your task on Earth and what you came down to do.

It is a task which all living creatures are working on, each within the limits of his or her own particular stage of development. A person who is not very high in intelligence and is of a lower state of evolution can only do what he can do. I can't do what Sathya Sai Baba does. I can't do what Jesus does. I can't do what Moses does. I can't do that. I can only do a little bit. All of us can only do what we can do, so be satisfied and stop grouching. Every being reawakened in spirit, a divine being identifying his or her consciousness with the Divine Being, has fulfilled his or her duty. When you pass on, you can say to yourself, "Well done," if you have spiritualized your life.

I have a letter here from someone who is a policeman.

> Today there was a riot in a court house jail. "Riot" sounds like a strong word, but this incident was just that. The jail has many cells. Each is about the size of a room, say 8x10, maybe a little smaller. Usually each cell has fifteen to twenty men in it. But today, each cell had twenty-five to thirty men. This is very unusual, but because of overload it sometimes happens.

> When these men first arrive, they are angry because they are in jail and restricted and because they are awakened at 4 a.m.

> They stay in the courthouse cells anywhere from ten to twelve hours, so you can understand how they feel. They have nothing to do but stand in a small cell for all that time. Since they are already angry, all it takes is one wrong look and trouble starts.

Can you imagine thirty men standing in such a small area for so long?

> So today it happened. Somebody got angry at somebody else. Words were exchanged and fists started flying. Because there was no room to fight, other men got punched and they punched back. The men in the other cells got angry and excited; fights broke out in each cell, one by one.

It jumped from cell to cell. Do you understand the power of negativity which some people call the devil or Satan?

> There are six cells in one cell block, and so there were about two hundred prisoners going at it. There is one captain and about six to ten officers assigned there, depending on lunch hours. In short, the jail is overloaded and understaffed. Ten officers can't stop a fight of two hundred men. Or can they?

> Looking at the whole scene, thoughts came into my mind. What should I do? Pray? Om? Ask a saint to intervene? Well, there isn't time to think of these things. The security sirens are put on, and the emergency security brigade charges in as the cell doors are opened. Bats, clubs

and guns are all ready for use.

No time to think. Just act. All the officers are tense and aggressive.

But you have always taught us to act with love. I followed your teaching. Instead of stepping forward, I stepped back. With my eyes open, I went into a trance and let forth all that love with which you have injected us, and here's what happened.

Immediately the screeching siren stopped, but the switch was still in place on 'On.' With the sudden stop of that noise, about eighty percent of the fighting stopped. Just like that.

I felt my eyes bulging with power as I began to expand and fill the whole place. I didn't care who saw this time because of the emergency.

He usually hides his spirituality down at the police station.

My eyes were wide open, but I didn't see with them after about three or four seconds. I spread out my arms and let go of the body.

You can visualize it, can't you? And he's a police officer.

When I came back, it was three minutes later and all the fighting had stopped. Later this morning, one of the officers said that one of the prisoners saw me, poked someone and told another, and another poked the next one and told the other, and they all started staring at me and got quiet.

Daniel in the lions' den. Do you understand how we can control things?

They said they never saw anyone in that position or with that kind of facial expression, and they lost all the power to fight.

I just know one thing you taught me — love. You say and show that love always saves, and I believe you. I still believe you. I will always believe you.

Have you spiritualized a bit of the Earth? How many times have you said, "Oh, I feel sick. Oh, I have a headache. This was a terrible day I had." That's not spiritualizing. You understand? That's not spiritualizing matter. That is cooperating with inertia.

When we spiritualize our bodies, Mother Earth gets spiritualized. We are little atoms of Mother Earth, and Mother Earth will not get spiritualized until we spiritualize ourselves.

Having identified our consciousness with the Divine Being, we have advanced the Earth's salvation, because Mother Earth is determined to spiritualize herself, and we are part of her. Our next step is to help others up the steps into the state of salvation. How many of you are having opportunities now to talk to others and help others? Don't proselytize, just give a little hint, once in a while, in a nice way. Learn the laws of the world, which are based on the laws of spirit which could not exist without Eternal Being.

The little things which identify us with this Earth plane of matter keep us bound to it. Anger is one thing that keeps us bound to this Earth. So make up your mind this moment that you're not going to be angry. Just say to yourself, "What is this to me? I follow Thee. I follow the way of truth. I follow the way of light."

I heard these words coming from above: "Wake up. Wake up. Take your rightful place as citizens of the world, the world intended by God, not this God-forsaken world of poverty, starvation, sin and lust."

God-forsaken, they say, because we have forsaken the Earth in pursuit of happiness and gratification for ourselves. Isn't that what's caused the Earth to go wrong? Wouldn't you say so? If you want your hair to stand up nicely, you spray your hair. You don't think it's going to damage the ozone layer, right? Think of all the little things we've done wrong, the little, tiny things that we don't think we're doing wrong. We have forsaken the Earth for the pursuit of happiness and gratification for ourselves and by acting as bickering children, bickering countries, and now bickering evangelists.

The wars on the horizon are only symbols of the fighting within us. When you fight down here, you're making a war. When a million people fight down here, you've got a big war — gangs, then countries fighting. It starts within us. All we can do to save our world and ourselves is to change and stop fighting. Forget your aspirations. Forget careers. Forget everything like that and just put everything into making yourself a perfect person from the tip of your toes to the top of your head.

I don't know whether I told you about the time when I experienced hysteria with that airplane. It was evening for us, but it was morning in Karachi, where a plane was being hijacked. I was home in my living room and I did not know what was happening, but all at once, I went mad. I had hysteria. I kept saying, "I'm going crazy, I'm going crazy, I've got hysteria, I'm going crazy." Then I'd say to the people in my house, "Don't listen to me, don't listen to me" because it was as if there were two of me, one at home and one tuning in with those people on that plane who were being lined up in the aisle, ready to be shot. Then I said, "I'm going to die, I'm going to die, I'm going to die." And I said, "Don't listen to me, don't listen to me, I'm not going to die." I had never experienced hysteria before, and I'm glad that I know hysteria now because I'm telling you, that is what is going to happen in the big cities — hysteria.

Satan has let loose his evil. Are you understanding this? You don't like the word Satan? Well, I'll say "the evil forces" then. Do you think there isn't a Satan? I've seen him. I told him I wondered why he was so ugly. I said, "What are you so ugly for? Why don't you be nice and be pretty?"

Yes, there is a Satan and he has let loose his evil upon the world. People do things they don't want to do and don't even know why they are doing them. Some of the people that you read about in the paper every day who have shot someone or have jumped out of windows, they didn't really want to do that. Something negative came over them and forced them to do it. Stay away from that! We are responsible unless we clean up the war within ourselves.

You must learn to be firm and strong in the midst of everything, so that if earthquakes are happening and people are screaming and yelling in the streets and running around like mad and a UFO comes over to rescue you, you can walk straight out in calmness, with love in your aura, and fearlessly walk into that beam of light from the UFO and be taken up. I want to teach you how to be firm and strong. I don't want you to learn it with your head, I want you to learn it with your heart, with your intuition. This is the only thing I'm going to teach — how to overcome yourselves and spiritualize this Mother Earth, and the glory of it all.

This is what we can do. Go deep within and look in. If there's anybody you've hated in this life at any time, anyone who has done dirt to you, forgive them because it's not worth hanging on to. If somebody's passed over, say, "Thank God, you've gone on to heaven and you're out of the mess." Start being positive. How can you know why God has chosen one of your beloveds to take them on to the other side? Maybe they're people who couldn't stand the hell that's down here. You follow?

There doesn't have to be hell. If you would pull yourself above the hell, there wouldn't be any hell. During World War II, I barely knew there was a war. I was sitting on my behind starting to meditate and do spiritual things. I never knew there was a lack of food. I never knew there was a lack of anything because there was always somebody bringing things to me into what I called my ashram, which was my studio. Why? I was in God-consciousness, and God is the source of all supply.

These little things which identify us with the Earth plane of matter keep us bound to it. The Master Jesus, or shall we call him Rabbi Jesus as the disciples did, said to his disciples, "What is this to thee? Follow thou me." Meaning, follow his teachings of truth and the way. Follow the truth, the light, the rock on which we can stand in the midst of the raging torrential floods of life here on Earth. No matter what happens to us, we can come through on that rock of truth, which is the same truth that Moses taught. There's only one truth, and we have to stand on it firmly from now on.

Children of God, Jesus laid it all out to his few innermost disciples to stay out of matter and come into spirit. Visualize these disciples, in their rags. They've just come from fishing, and he said, "Come with me," and they didn't say, "I've got to go back and tell my wife, my children." Feel it inside. He was this wonderful being of light and he said, "Follow me," and they followed him.

As they were walking, he would stop in a place and they would all have a nice talk. That's where they are right this moment. Let's read Mark, Chapter 13:

> And as he went out of the temple, one of his disciples saith unto him, "Master, see what manner of stones and what buildings are here!" And Jesus answering said unto him, "Seest thou these great buildings? There shall not be left one stone upon another, that shall not be thrown down." And as he sat upon the Mount of Olives over against the temple, Peter and James and John and Andrew asked him privately, "Tell us, when shall these things be, and what shall be the sign when all these things shall be fulfilled?" And Jesus answering them began to say, "Take heed lest any man deceive you, for many shall come in my name saying, 'I am Christ,' and shall deceive many. And when ye shall hear of wars and rumors of wars, be ye not troubled, for such things must needs be; but the end shall

not be yet. For nation shall rise against nation, and kingdom against kingdom, and there shall be earthquakes in
divers places, and there shall be famines and troubles:
these are the beginnings of sorrows."

But what did Jesus say? "Be ye not troubled." See that your name gets
written in the Book of Life. The Book of Life is the record of our life's actions,
both good and bad. When the soul comes out of worldliness it will be
reflected in the Book of Life and the soul will be enabled to pass onto the
next stage of development. That's what I'm here for — to see we get our
names written in. Do you follow this? These things can happen, but we can
come through without fear. Fear is the worst thing possible because it starts
a whole ball rolling of what's going to happen that never happens. Develop
your intuition, then you'll be in the right place at the right time. The day
an earthquake is going to happen in New York City, you'll say, "Hey, I think
I'll go for a ride in the country today." And you won't be here. We must
build up a faith and believe that we are taken care of. This is what I want to
build up in you — and then things will go right.

"There shall not be left one stone upon another," Jesus said. I know there
will not be a stone left of New York City. We may come to this cathedral two
thousand years from now and see some ruins here, and walk in and say,
"You know, this feels a little like I've been here before. What kind of place
is this?" "Oh, in those days it was called a church." "Oh, what was a
church?" "It was a place where people met to love God." "What a funny
thing, I thought you loved God all the time, outside under the trees and
everywhere."

Mother Earth is going to do what she wants to do and you can't stop it,
not one of you. So you might as well work with her and spiritualize your
part — your body. If those around you won't get spiritualized, just shut
your mouth.

Tonight I want to talk for a few minutes on what is coming. In the past
five months, I've been shown many things. I saw a vision, just a quick vision.
I saw a horse prancing, a white horse's foot prancing, ready to go, as if at
the starting gate. The white horse is the sign of the breaking of the first seal
spoken of in Revelations[2] that signals the beginning of the end of things as
we know them. It's prancing to go, ready to shoot off. Do you follow this?

I want you to know these things not with your brain, but with your heart.
Haven't I been telling you for five years what would happen if we didn't

change our ways? The ozone layer is broken now, as I predicted. The hole is as big as the United States and, they say, as high as Mount Everest — and they don't know what to do. If it spreads all over the Earth, well, we can say goodbye to all of us.

Nostradamus appeared to me in the night and said the time will come when for a while we will be able to go out only at night, never under the sun, or we will be burned because of the higher intensity of the ultraviolet rays.

We humans have caused this situation with our chemicals, with our sprays, with all these things. We are responsible for this and for many other things that are destroying our Earth. We already can see the signs of what the Earth plane is going through. Even the dullest clucks can see and are getting worried.

Near our place, Con Edison had dug a great big square trench the size of a car. My bedroom was right above it, and all night long I could hear the cars screeching. Unfortunately, one didn't make it — clink, clink, bang — and the ambulance came. Apparently they had forgotten to put the red warning flag up.

Now if there is a pothole and there is a red flag to warn drivers, would you think the red flag is negative or positive? Positive, of course. Was God negative or positive when He warned Noah that a great storm was brewing and that he should build an ark? Of course, He was positive, and therefore we now exist, all of us, because Noah preserved life on Earth. You think you're Jewish? You think you're Christian? We're just offspring of Noah. I don't know what religion he was.

Was Moses positive or negative when he threatened the Pharaoh with a plague? Was he negative or positive when he warned the Jews to go inside their houses, close the doors, and put the mark of the lamb's blood on their doorposts? Isn't that interesting, the lamb's blood? All through the Bible it says the lamb is going to be slaughtered — that means Jesus on the cross. Moses said to put the lamb's blood on the door and not to worry. Trust God! I can just hear the grumbling that went on that night: "That old Moses, he's always telling us that we're going to be free. Now he says we have to go in and lock our doors." Do you think he was positive or negative in warning them to go inside and shut their doors?

Was it positive or negative when God was so kind as to inform Daniel what would come on Earth if the people of the Earth did not change their ways? When he heard it, even Daniel said he was scared. His words were, "My thoughts alarm me," but he kept the matter in hand. I too will keep the matter in hand. If you haven't used the Bible lately, dust it off and read Daniel, Chapter 12, Verses 1-4.

> And at that time shall Michael stand up, the great prince which standeth for the children of thy people; and there shall be a time of trouble, such as never was since there was a nation even to that same time; and at that time thy people shall be delivered, everyone that shall be found written in the book.

What Daniel says here is the same as what John says later, "everyone written in the book." Be assured those books are open and being written in. We want to get some of it erased and rewritten. That is what I'm going to show you how to do.

> And many of them that sleep in the dust of the earth shall awake, some to everlasting life, and some to shame and everlasting contempt. And they that be wise shall shine as the brightness of the firmament; and they that turn many to righteousness as the stars forever and ever. But thou, O Daniel, shut up the words, and seal the book, even to the time of the end; many shall run to and fro, and knowledge shall be increased.

Knowledge certainly increased, didn't it? We learned how to blow up cities with the bomb. We know how to spray food with chemicals. Very smart, aren't we? Knowledge has increased greatly since that time — a little bit too much.

What I would like to talk about now is the three days of darkness that Padre Pio speaks about. This is a warning or a red flag like Daniel's and Moses'.

Jesus, talking to his disciples, said that immediately after the tribulation of these days the sun will be darkened, the moon will not give off light, the stars will fall from heaven, and the powers of heaven shall be shaken. Now is it negative or positive for me to tell you what to do during the three days of darkness? If I don't tell you and the three days of darkness come and you are inside your house, not knowing whether the sun will ever come out again, you will begin to go berserk and say that the end of the world has come. "Look what's happened! The moon hasn't come out, the sun

hasn't come out, stars are falling. Good God, the end of the world has come."
But if you know what's going to happen, you know that at the end of three
days, you can open your door, and the sun will be shining and everything
will be beautiful.

Isn't it better that I tell you about it, so you can act like human beings?
It's going to come. I have no idea what will cause it, but it may be a comet
— they use fancy words in the Bible about stars falling. What you have to
do when the time comes is put aside some water for drinking and have
plenty of blankets. It's going to be cold because there will be no sun for three
days. You won't be able to cook, so you'll need food, canned goods that you
don't need to cook, that you can just eat — for three days only. Don't look
outside because God doesn't want you to see what's happening outside.

Now is this positive or negative? Of course it's positive. Anyone who
thinks it's negative is cuckoo. Double cuckoo. Because you would go crazy.
Nostradamus said that if you go out during this time, you'll be bones, white
bones. But if you wait, by the time you go out, it will all be cleaned up. How
it will be cleaned up I don't know. But I have faith in angels. I have faith in
the UFOs. I have faith in God Almighty. They know how to clean up the
world, and they will clean it up before we look at it. Do you understand
this? Did not Moses tell his people to go in and stay in and the plague would
pass over them? That's what Padre Pio is telling us. I think we all respect
Padre Pio. I have a picture of a girl who has no pupils in her eyes. She prayed
so hard that he healed her, and now she can see like a normal person,
although she still has no pupils.

The following is a translation of a letter, "A personal letter written by
Padre Pio addressed to the Commission of Heroldsbach appointed by the
Vatican which testifies to the truth and reality of these revelations given by
Our Lord to Padre Pio, the Capuchin priest who bore the stigmata." These
are Jesus' words to him.

January 23, 1950

> Pray! Make reparations. Be fervent and practice mortifi-
> cation.

That is, the denial of the lesser self.

> Great things are at stake! Pray! Men are running toward
> the abyss of Hell in great rejoicing and merry-making, as
> though they were going to a masquerade ball or the wed-
> ding feast of the devil himself. Assist Me in the salvation

of souls. The measure of sin is filled! The day of revenge, with its terrifying happenings is near! — Nearer than you can imagine! And the world is sleeping in false security! The Divine Judgment shall strike them like a thunderbolt! This godless and wicked people shall be destroyed without mercy, as were the inhabitants of Sodom and Gomorrah of old. Yes, I tell you, their wickedness was not as great at that time as that of our human race of today!

January 28

Keep your windows well covered.

Did you hear that? If you have no curtains, take some blankets and hammer them up with a nail. Got it? So that you can't look out.

Do not look out. Light a blessed candle which will suffice for many days.

Flashlights will do, too.

Pray continually. Read spiritual books. Make acts of Spiritual Communion, also acts of love which are so pleasing to Us. Pray...in order that many souls may be saved. Do not go outside the house.

Provide yourself with sufficient food. The powers of nature shall be moved and a rain of fire shall make people tremble with fear. Have courage!

Are you going to tremble? No, you're not going to.

Have courage! I am in the midst of you.

February 7

Take care of the animals during these days...Punishment will bear witness to the times. My angels, who are to be the executioners of this work, are ready with their pointed swords. They will take special care to annihilate all those who mocked me and would not believe in My revelations.

Hurricanes of fire will pour forth from the clouds and spread over the entire earth! Storms, bad weather, thunderbolts and earthquakes will cover the earth for two days.

This is what will come first. Before the cold night comes, the sun will go down in the middle of the day. So if you're in your office typing, just say, "Excuse me, I'm going to the bathroom," and don't come back. Go home. Do you understand? Don't try to go miles up to the country, just go to the closest place where your friends are, go in and cuddle in for three days. You're always complaining you have no rest — you have three days of rest coming.

> An uninterrupted rain of fire will take place! It will begin during a very cold night. All this is to prove that God is the Master of Creation.

> Those who hope in Me, and believe in My words, have nothing to fear because I will not forsake them, nor those who spread My message. No harm will come to those who are in the state of grace and who seek My Mother's protection.

> That you may be prepared for these visitations, I will give you the following signs and instructions: The night will be very cold. The wind will roar.

Memorize it. Let it go down in the subconscious. But every cold night, don't think it's the night.

> After a time, thunderbolts will be heard. Lock all the doors and windows. Talk to no one outside the house.

Somebody will come knocking late. Are you going to open the door or not? It will be the hardest time of your life when some relative comes knocking at the door too late. If you open that door, everybody inside will be annihilated. If a knock comes at the door, don't open it, don't look out to see who it is.[3]

> Kneel down...be sorry for your sins, and beg My Mother's protection. Do not look during the earthquake, because the anger of God is holy!...

> Those who disregard this advice will be killed instantly. The wind will carry with it poisonous gases which will be diffused over the entire earth. Those who suffer and die innocently will be martyrs and they will be with Me in My Kingdom.

> Satan will triumph! But in three nights, the earthquake and fire will cease. On the following day the sun will shine again, angels will descend from Heaven and will spread the spirit of peace over the earth. A feeling of immeasurable gratitude will take possession of those who survive this most terrible ordeal... with which God has visited the earth

since creation. This catastrophe shall come upon the earth like a flash of lightning at which moment the light of the morning sun shall be replaced by black darkness.

No one shall leave the house or look out of a window from that moment on. I Myself shall come amidst thunder and lightning. The wicked shall behold My Divine Heart. There shall be great confusion because of this utter darkness in which the entire earth shall be enveloped, and many, many shall die from fear and despair. Are you going to be one of those? You're not going to die from fear! That would be a stupid thing.

Those who shall fight for My cause shall receive grace from My Divine Heart; and the cry, "Who is like unto God!" shall serve as a means of protection to many. However, many shall burn in the fields like withered grass! The godless shall be annihilated, so that afterwards the just shall be able to start afresh.

On the day, as soon as complete darkness has set in, no one shall leave the house or look out of the window. The darkness shall last a day and a night, followed by another day and a night, and another day — but on the night following, the stars will shine again, and on the next morning the sun shall rise again, and it will be springtime!

In the days of darkness, My elect shall not sleep, as did the disciples in the Garden of Olives. They shall pray incessantly, and they shall not be disappointed in Me. I shall gather My elect. Hell will believe itself to be in possession of the entire earth, but I shall reclaim it!

Do you, perhaps, think that I would permit My Father to have such terrible chastisements come upon the world, if the world would turn from iniquity to justice? But because of My great love, these afflictions shall be permitted to come upon man. Although many may curse Me, yet thousands of souls shall be saved through them. No human understanding can fathom the depth of My love!

Pray! Pray! I desire your prayers. My Dear Mother Mary, Saint Joseph, Saint Elizabeth, Saint Conrad, Saint Michael,

Saint Peter, the little Therese...

And we should add Moses and Elijah, who shall be with Jesus at this time.

> ...shall be your intercessors. Implore their aid! Be coura-
> geous soldiers of Christ! At the return of light, let everyone
> give thanks...for Their protection! The devastation shall be
> very great! But I, Your God, will have purified the earth. I
> am with you. Have confidence!

Is that positive or negative? See, there are a lot of Pollyannas around who say, "Oh, we shouldn't talk anything negative. We should all talk very positive." But if Moses hadn't told them to go into their houses and close their doors, the Jewish people would have been wiped out right then and there. So if they say not to leave your house at that time, if Nostradamus cares enough to come down and tell me things, I call it positive, because it'll make us aware.

Get it into your souls. For ten years you've been getting it into your heads here. Now I want you to get it into your souls and to start living it. You say, "Oh sure, Hilda gave a great talk tonight. Oh, it was on this and that." Then the next day you forget what it was. Now you have to start living it. We have very little time left. That horse is pawing. Here we go. Knowing all this, we must always keep in mind the outcome — the glory we shall live to see and love.

Don't dwell on the negative, but dwell on what the outcome will be. I'm getting silly images. I'm seeing a piece of material, and a person is cutting out a dress. It looks like nothing. When the person has sewn it up and put a pleat here and a pleat there, it comes out beautifully. We've got to see what's going to come out of all this. Sure, we have to go through it. When a woman gets pregnant and she is in the ninth month, she can't get out of it. She can't say, "Well, I've decided not to go through with this. I've changed my mind." We can't change our minds. Mother Earth is not going to change her mind — she is going to change her geography. We want to be in the right place.

Nobody's going to be annihilated. If thugs and bad men and women came into a peaceful meeting, they would be asked to be peaceful or leave, would they not? That is what this time to come is all about. The sinners, the bad ones, will be asked to go to another world where they can be as rowdy and greedy as they want and make each other as miserable as they want, until they can see their mistakes. Then they will be invited back at the right time, having learned the difference between right and wrong. Is that clear? Nobody's going to be annihilated. They'll go to another planet about equal to what our planet is now.

I want to read you something now that has been given us by the Masters.

The hour is late. The sun is setting.

Cannot you see the signs that are so clearly laid out for you? The earthquakes, the mudslides, the volcanoes, the eruptions, the drugs taking over, the suicides? How much more clearly do you want God to spell out the handwriting on the wall, kids? Look around and wake up out of your lethargy. What does God want of you? You, His child as an individual — what does He want of you?

He sent you to Earth from heaven. He allowed you to come to this school called Earth to learn peace in the midst of chaos. He sent you to learn to be true to yourself and your God when all those around you are floundering in the mud that sucks them under like quicksand.

We must learn to control everything — the animal instincts within us, the one that would want to punch somebody in the nose, the one who would say this is unrighteous, the one who gets angry, the one who holds on to all the anger that's happened in this world. We've got to overcome it. As Jesus says, "What is that to thee? Follow thou Me." Everywhere are the sirens — not the sirens on the cars, but the sirens who call to us as they did to the ancient sailors and Ulysses. The sirens of dope, prostitution, alcohol, and lustful ways pull you off your course if you do not stand tall and firm, centered in your Self. And who is your Self? Think inside, who is your Self? You are that wonderful flame of light.

What does God want of you? God wants you to turn about, start walking the narrow razor's edge path of righteousness because maybe we have only twelve years. And maybe we haven't even got that, maybe we've got about four years. Maybe we've got one. Maybe we've got one month. Maybe we've got one night. We don't know when it's going to happen. They're keeping it a secret, those blokes up there. Do you know why? Otherwise we'd say, "Oh gee, we've got five years. I can go to the discotheques now, get into that heavy music. What difference does it make? I'll start in four years." But they keep it a secret. So we have to start right now to build ourselves up. Stop short the littleness of you. Have you littleness in you? Little itsy bitsy rot rotting you away inside? Like cankers in your mouth?

Be ready for the sunrise. The warmth of it will caress you

and dry the tears of remorse for having strayed from your
path.

If you could only have remorse, kids! If you come to the place where
remorse can come in, say, "Oh God, what a rotter I was." Just for a second.
"Oh God, what a rotter I was. How mean I was, how rotten!" And you
repent. At that moment, it gets released and wiped out of your book. If you
could only do that! But you hang on there and you don't have remorse. You
say, "He did it. She did it. If I hadn't met that person, I wouldn't have done
that. My mother did it. My father did it. My grandmother did it. My children
did it." Always somebody else outside yourself instead of looking into
yourself and saying, "What a lousy boob I am. I have remorse, God."

We shouldn't be so blasé as to think we can go through life just as we
have been. We've got to change, change, change, change, change. If you
think you're so perfect that you don't need to change, then you better get
rid of your ego.

Be fearless warriors of God. Be true to Him. God sent you. God sent Jesus
to the Earth to train you and warn you of the pitfalls. Wasn't that nice of
God to take hold of Jesus? And wasn't it darn nice of Jesus to come down
to this stinkpot? Wasn't it nice of all of us to come down to this stinkpot to
do this work that we have to do from now on?

Have you not fallen into enough pitfalls and been bruised and hurt
enough? Haven't you been hurt enough, or do you want to be hurt some
more? Well, I'm telling you, you'll get a great big hurt if you don't change.
Have you not suffered enough with unworthiness and self-defacement?
The flame, oh, the flame, the spark within you remembers your vow to your
Father/Mother God to come to Earth to clean it up and help build it into a
paradise.

And what did we do? As soon as we got down here, we fell into gangs,
we fell into groups at school where they're doing this and that and saying,
"You want to come to a party? They're smoking a little stuff." We thought,
oh, that won't hurt, I'm bigger than that. So we fell and forgot what we came
down for. Now I'm reminding you what we really came down here for.

This is what we can do: we can change. When you have a daughter who
is angry at you and you're about to get angry at her, don't say, "I have a
daughter who's angry at me," reinforcing the negative. What you do is you
sit down for half an hour a day and affirm the positive by saying, "The God
in her loves the God in me and the God in me loves the God in her. The God

in her loves the God in me and the God in me loves the God in her." Then when you meet her, you give her a big smile. If it hasn't worked, you work harder at it. Why suffer more and bring suffering on others? God loves you. Jesus forgives you.

Turn about now before the sun rises on the Age of God, the Age of Truth, so that you can be there and look into the sun full gaze. The light within you dims the brightness of the sun.

Yes, yes, I say again and again, be fearless warriors of God. Help build this age of love brick by brick. What are these bricks? We are — yes, we are the bricks, and we must be smooth, clean, beautiful, golden bricks. That means we must say "Stop!" with determination and inner power to our lower personalities so that they don't rule us. We must live as we truly are, in accord with our higher Self with its divine ideals.

We can say "Stop!" when we start going down into negation, can't we? But if some karma has to be paid off and you start getting a bit of sickness, say, "Well, God, this will pay off a bit of my karma." Don't moan and groan, but stick it out.

There's no longer room on Earth for self-deluding hypocrites. We must live what we talk, live that which we believe in. If that student of mine who's a policeman hadn't believed in the love that I had given him and put his hands out and gone into trance, there would have been a lot of people who would have been killed that day in the prison. Then we would have seen it in the paper. We didn't see anything in the paper about him putting his hands out and going to God, did we? They never put that in.

The Masters are asking, when are we going to spiritualize the Earth-matter plane? It means we don't get angry any more. We aren't petty. We forget what that man or that woman did to us ten years ago or twenty years ago. We don't hold a grudge. We say, "Oh, let that water go under the bridge." Why? To spiritualize the Earth plane so that the vibrations of Heaven shall descend upon the Earth.

Thrice in my life I have experienced levitation. I don't say that I hit the ceiling, but I went up a little way, a foot. Once I had my arms out and I was talking as if I were the Divine Mother. I was talking out of this glory, and all at once I felt every atom of me was changing into spiritual atoms, no longer matter. Fernandez, who came to my classes, used to kind of audit everything and see that everybody's head was up and not nodding from boredom. He looked at me, and I opened my eyes and I looked at him. I knew my atoms were being spiritualized and I was going to go up, and when you kids opened your eyes, I would not be there. So I looked at him and he stared at me, and I said, "Well, let's everybody come down now. Open your eyes, and let's sing 'Glory be to God.' Come on down." Another time, when I was dancing, before I went to India, I felt myself go up and people saw me go off the floor. Another time, I was walking home saying the name of God and I began to float up off the sidewalk and had to hold on to the buildings. So I know it's possible. I know these bodies can become spiritualized and can be raised up. Those are the bodies that are going up in the Rapture. I also think that the UFOs will come and take the rest of us who can't quite make our bodies go into that much rapture. But you've got to have something in order to walk into that light.

When I was in the country with a group of people and a UFO came, two of my students wanted to go and touch the beings who had walked out of the UFO. These students' legs were shaking and they couldn't stop them because the vibration of those beings was so high. Their insides were jumping up and down. Why? Because we're so stupidly negative. But we're not going to be that way any more, because we're going to be reborn. We're going to be reborn into a new consciousness — a wonderful new consciousness.

Saint John talks of this in Revelations, Chapter 21. On the island in Greece he was shown a vision, and this is what he saw:

> And I saw a new heaven and a new earth: for the first heaven and the first earth were passed away; and there was no more sea. And I, John, saw the holy city, new Jerusalem, coming down from God out of Heaven...And I heard a great voice out of heaven saying, "Behold, the tabernacle of God is with men, and he will dwell with them, and they shall be his people, and God himself shall be with them, and be their God. And God shall wipe away all tears from their eyes; and there shall be no more death, neither sorrow, nor crying, neither shall there be any more pain: for the former things are passed away."
>
> And he that sat upon the throne said, "Behold, I make all things new." And he said unto me, "Write: for these words are true and faithful." And he said unto me, "It is

done. I am the Alpha and the Omega, the beginning and the end. I will give unto him that is athirst of the fountain of the waters of life freely. He that overcometh shall inherit all things; and I shall be his God, and he shall be my son [and daughter]. But the fearful, and the unbelieving, and the abominable, and the murderers, and the whore-mongers, and the sorcerers, and the idolaters, and all liars, shall have their part in the lake which burneth with fire and brimstone..."

And there came unto me one of the seven angels...saying, "Come hither, I will show thee..." And he carried me away in the spirit to a great and high mountain, and showed me that great city, the holy Jerusalem, descending out of heaven from God, having the glory of God: and her light was like unto a stone most precious, even like a jasper stone, clear as crystal...And I saw no temple therein: for the Lord God Almighty and the Lamb are the temple of it. And the city had no need of the sun, neither of the moon, to shine in it: for the glory of God did lighten it, and the Lamb is the light thereof.

And the nations of them which are saved shall walk in the light of it: and the kings of the earth do bring their glory and honor into it...And there shall in no wise enter into it any thing that defileth, neither whatsoever worketh abomination, or maketh a lie: but they which are written in the Lamb's book of life...And he saith unto me..."I am the Alpha and Omega, the beginning and the end, the first and the last."

Who is God depending on to enable these prophecies to be fulfilled, to make this come to pass, this Jerusalem to come down? On us! Say, "Me!" It's on each one of you He's depending.

The Scriptures will be fulfilled by those brave enough to dedicate themselves to His service of love. They're going to be fulfilled by you people.

Our bodies, minds and feelings must be spiritualized and they must harmonize. Usually our mind is way off somewhere else. How many have gone home and come back since you've been here? Did you have a good time? How was your house? Or did you go over and eat at a restaurant?

See? You can't even control your mind and keep it on God in here.

Will you do the simple things necessary? Will you try hard this month? Oh, you'll fail every day. At the end of the day when you lay down to sleep, say to yourself, "Let me see. Where did I fail? I failed there. I was so damn rude there, and I spoke so mean there. I said no to that person there," and then see yourself relive it — doing it right. We must make the air clean and wonderful each night.

Will you do the simple things necessary? So simple, so little. Just trust God through all troubles. Keep your mind stayed on your goal through thick and thin. Be alert to the jabs of the devil's negative thoughts coming through your own mind or from another's, trying to drag you down. The devil is ready to pounce at any moment when you are off guard. Be on guard like a soldier on duty. Be on guard all the time.

Now, here's the wonderful part. Step over your lower self. I've spoken of this great big consciousness, oh so big, of the Kingdom of God, of the Garden of Eden, that Jesus is talking about — the Way, the Truth, the Light. Down here are all these little rocks of our petty, little rotten old self. Step over them into the Kingdom. There you don't feel mean or petty. When you get petty, push yourself back in again as fast as possible. Say, "My God, let me get back into the Kingdom again." Know what the reward is for you.

Let me read to you what I have been shown of the New Age of Truth about to dawn. Do you want to know what it's going to be like? Then you'll know it's worth working for.

This is the vision I had of what is to come in the New Age of God, when we all get rid of our junk. You can't enter it with your junk. That's one rule. You go to the door and they say, "Have you got a suitcase? Sorry, you can't come in." You've got to go empty-handed.

This is the future world: We of the new time to come will be born conscious of the eternal flame within, and will not have to undo a millennium of animal instincts or prejudices. We will not be told incessantly that we will have to go out and earn a living. Nobody will have money. Life will be completely devoted to living the truth naturally, without striving, each of us according to our own capacity and intended talents. The compensation will be the feeling of completion, bringing joy within. There will be no deluge of musts and must nots. There will only be the immediate sad awareness of not having listened to the right note within, the intuition.

We will not be tormented with the urgency of job hunting, being a success, out-ranking others, or trying for A's, for nobody succeeds or fails in the land of the future. Success is to be in accord with the eternal Self within, the pure flame of divine love. We will not depend on a teacher, a book or a machine. The Book of Life within will be open to all, and that brings all knowledge effortlessly, opens us to discovery and to experiencing.

We will cultivate the powers within the body and mind. Our perception and comprehension, which are not from books, will be fostered as a vision of dreams of other worlds. This vision will build and prepare direct communication and open subtle senses long held captive within.

If machines, in the beginning, are used in the city of tomorrow, they will only be used for a short time until we develop in our own hearts the source of the pure power, which will one day transmute matter. The power of thought, which was used by a very few high initiates of Egypt to raise the huge stones of the pyramids, will become common knowledge for us all. There will no longer be evil ones to misuse God's glorious energy. He can at last entrust to us His secrets to make the perfect world for His perfect children.

We will be taught by the great teachers to release the dormant gifts, the true and potent power, the book of knowledge that creates, that changes everything. We will be taught to recognize our own powers and we will believe and know the power of truth. The purer and clearer we become, the more in harmony with the laws, the more matter responds to the truth. Then the world will become spiritualized. For everything is actually possible and there is no impossibility except as we believe it to be so.

We will have no screens. We will be free of "you," "me," "yours," "mine." We will have no mental barriers, for we will be able to know each other's thoughts without words.

We will at last consciously know what we have unconsciously known since the beginning of time. We will recognize the same flame everywhere, in everyone and everything.

There will be no more boundaries inside or outside. No more "I want" or "I take." Wars will have ceased, for there will be no war within us. There will be no more tensions of time. Therefore, our bodies will be healthy, happy and free to live for hundreds of years.

There will be no more lonely selves, for completion will be within, the harmony in thousands of bodies making a great symphony of life. Every single movement of ours, every second will be perfect, every act true. Every word will be exact, words flowing rhythmically as poetry from our lips. In this way truth will mold matter and spiritualize it. Our world will at last take its rightful place in the universe, sending out light rays unbeknownst to ourselves.

Isn't it worth working for? We just have to give up our little petty selves. We haven't much to give up — just a little bit of that personality so we can let the other person be right even if they're wrong.

Prepare yourself. Give up your old self. Come out of your cocoon and see who you are. You're not an ugly worm in a cocoon. You're a butterfly that's come out — a butterfly! You have to realize it now. After years of coming to these classes, you've got to know it. Let the mind which was in Jesus, God's mind, be in you. What would he think about it all? He would not be afraid. He said, "Tear down this temple and I'll build it up in three days." They thought he was talking about the temple they were standing in. The temple he was talking about was his own body. He wasn't afraid. He built it up again in three days. Do you follow? He had no fear. When Lazarus was dead, they said, "Oh, you've come too late, Master." But he said, "Get out of the way. Step aside. Roll back the rock." And Lazarus came out. Jesus kept his mind positive.

We can do anything, kids, if we believe. You've got to have belief in yourself. You've got to have belief that you can. You've got to stop all your stupid ways. You've got to stop being negative and start loving.

I would like to tell you about the first time that I saw Christ as God. It was before I went to India. I'd met him already. I'd gone through a kind of ceremony with him in which he took me as his own. He had said, "Give me all your time." All those things I'd done, and yet I still didn't know. One day I just saw him, and there was God — because there wasn't a thing in him that wasn't the same as God. There wasn't a thing in Moses that wasn't the same as God, or he couldn't have led his people as he did. There's not a thing in Skanda that isn't the same as God. And there's not a thing in us, in our true Self, that is not the same as God. Do you understand that? Do you truly? Only, what do we do? We put all this junk around us of negation that we've learned for so long.

It's so heartbreaking for me that we just don't take the bull by the horns and say, "I am going to be reborn. I want to be reborn." If those Christians on TV can get reborn, can't we get reborn? To be reborn is to go into a new consciousness.

I see it like this: there's a great big universe, and in that universe is perfection. Down here is a lot of rubble and junk, and our little old miserable, material self. When you step out of the worldly muck into a new consciousness, you change. If you're a smoker, smoking drops off. If you're an alcoholic, drinking drops off, because there is no alcohol in that kingdom. If you're a prostitute, that drops off. If you're a sinner, that drops off.

Ramakrishna had cancer of the throat. Do you think he was a mediocre person? No, he had it for other people. He paid the price of their karma. Ramana Maharshi had cancer of the arm. A woman asked in meditation, "How can my guru be so low as to get cancer?" and then she saw the face of humanity. He took it on for humanity, kids.

This is where I can't talk because I cry. What shall I do? I don't know how to talk without crying. I love God so much that when I even speak of Jesus or God I cry. That's why I don't like to come here and talk about it. You see, Jesus didn't have to go on that cross, with those two bums beside him. He said that a myriad of angels could waft him away. But he put his hands out and let the nails go in. Who did he do it for? Who? For us! And that blood of his, which was divine blood, fell.

If we believe, then all these things which we call sins, that block our minds, will drop away. When you begin to think, "I am a sinner," say, "No, Jesus already took that away in the great kingdom of the universe." When you start thinking, "I'm unworthy," say, "No, it's not true. He went on that cross for me to take unworthiness away. He's taken it away if I believe. But if I don't believe, then I'm out here with the rocky self."

Can you get the picture of being reborn? You go to say a nasty negative thing and you think, "No, that's not true. I'm not sick or nasty because Jesus took my sickness and nastiness away." If you've got sickness tonight, give it up. If you've got a feeling of unworthiness in you, look inside right now and see what unworthiness you have. Step over the rubble and go in there to that great kingdom — call it the Garden of Eden, if you want, or the consciousness of Christ — and say, "I'm forgiven. I don't hold onto it any more. It's not in my consciousness. I am love."

If there's anyone you still hate, oh please, let go of that hatred this night. I don't want you to be out there in those three days of darkness. Please, does it do you any good to keep hate in your heart? I beg of you, step over and say, "No, I don't have any hate. I'm in the kingdom. I'm reborn this moment into a new consciousness of glory."

If there's anything you've done for which you hate yourself, anything that at the time you were doing it, something in your consciousness said, "This is not right. I know I shouldn't do this, but everybody is doing it" — give it up this night. Step over into that great kingdom and say, "It's wiped out. It's forgiven this moment. It's wiped out."

Please get out of your heads and into your hearts. Believe in your heart. Believe that cigarette smoking can drop off this moment because you're not in the consciousness of it any more. If alcohol is your problem, it'll taste so bad that you won't want to take it. If it's crack, whatever it is, anything you feel you're doing wrong or saying wrong, step into that great big universe of the consciousness of God, of Christ, and know that the debt has been paid off.

If somebody came to you and said, "I paid your debt off. You owed $100 and I paid it," would you say, "Oh no, it can't be, you haven't paid it off"? How stupid would you be? Your debt's paid off, kids, if you go into the new consciousness.

Open up this moment into love. If there's anyone you don't love, say, "Jesus, will you jump into my heart and love for me?" Even on the cross, he turned to the man on a cross next to him and said, "You will be in heaven with me." He said, "Father, forgive them. They know not what they do." If somebody's been mean to you, they didn't know what they were doing to you. If you were mean to someone, you didn't know what you were doing to them.

Look into yourself now to see if there's anything negative left. Be free. Walk out of here a free soul, calling yourself reborn if you want to, if you like those words. Reborn into what? Into a new way of thinking, a new way of feeling.

Look into yourself now. Do you have any hate left? Then say, "Please, oh God, wipe me clear of it." If you did any wrongs that you felt were sinful — or maybe they were just experiences, but because you weren't one with God, you thought they were sinful — step into this consciousness and let these wrongs drop out of your mind and out of your subconscious. The next time they come back, say, "No, get away from me. I'm reborn into a new consciousness, a consciousness of belief that my golden book is open and whatever is negative can be erased and rewritten."

If you have ever been scared stiff, if somebody was chasing you or whatever, I want you this moment to relive it. Go back and relive it without fear. Why didn't Daniel get eaten by the lions? Because he wasn't afraid. He was in the consciousness of God, and the lions couldn't come at him. He had no animal left in him.

I'm going to close now. If anybody wants a special prayer for themselves, just let them stand, and the others who are sitting, pray hard for them. Don't be ashamed to stand, because there's not one here who can throw a stone at you, not one. I'm going to ask the Holy Spirit to come down on you wherever you are. I'm going to ask that the heavens open up. Whatever it is that's in your heart, the Holy Spirit, the Holy Ghost, the Comforter that Jesus said he would leave with us, will flow down on us now. Don't take it for granted. I will not stop until I feel that breeze, that breath of the Holy Spirit come down upon us.

Please, Jesus, send that Holy Spirit upon these people that they may walk out of here free and reborn in a new consciousness. The old shall leave them.

The Masters told me to give this benediction to you: "Love shall be your way." We will work out our problems with love and kindness. We shall be Children of God and Sons and Daughters of Light. We belong to a New Age of God to come, and we shall come through victorious and strong and whole.

Please let that Holy Spirit come and blow upon us. Oh, send the Comforter into the heart of each one of those standing. The rest of you sitting, pray hard for them that everything up to this moment shall be wiped out of their minds and they shall be reborn like little children coming out of a womb. If the other thoughts come back, say, "No, the Holy Spirit took them away from me. Oh God, I am a Son of God, I am a Daughter of Light. I belong in that New Age of God, Jesus. Oh Lords of Karma, rewrite the book and the things I've done wrong. Wipe them out for me, please. Write in the good. Oh God, Eternal One, Eternal One."

Just stand and love God with all your heart and feel the coolness come down upon you. Believe that it is the Comforter, and believe it will cleanse your blood and cleanse you of everything. If smoking is a problem, oh God, take it from him or her. If alcohol is a problem, please let it drop off so it is no longer wanted or remembered.

Believe in your heart now, all of you who stood up, that the Masters will watch your development. They are watching you every moment from the time you get up in the morning till you go to sleep at night — and even at night you can go and learn from them.

Feel yourselves consecrated. Oh, glory be! I thank You, Lord, that You have heard us.

Feel new. Feel reborn.

Be new people in God, new people in Christ.

Chapter Two

The Real You

I want your minds to be aware of what's going to happen, so that you will be prepared to be strong, whole, vibrant people, depending on God Almighty rather than just being pushed around and shoved around. Unless you understand what is happening, you will be hysterical at what will come upon this Earth.

I want to start to really make you tough. Is that okay with you? That is why, before I start my lecture each month, I give you a potpourri of anything I've been thinking about since I saw you last. People send me newspaper clippings, and I bring them to your attention so your minds will be aware of what's going on.

When I was living out in Santa Barbara, I knew a Buddhist priest named Bukan Saramsa. When I came back to Oakland, there he was in the middle of the street, coming along with his long whiskers and ocher robe. He stopped me and said, "The time will come when hordes like wolves will come down into the city and go at the people." Well, it has started now. Do you understand? We are going to pray that God will protect us. This is not my lecture, this is just a little introduction to give you some guts in this world. All the sweet singing, all the mantras in the world are not going to help you. You've got to get strong inside with love. You can come through if you can hold your head together and your heart together. That's why I want you to know what's happening on the Earth.

Did you read the newspaper? A man was going across the street. A van came around and almost hit him. He just gave the van a pat. The driver got out and gave him a shove. He gave a shove back. The driver took out a knife and thrust it into his throat, and the man was dead. I say to you people here, every one of you, don't say anything back to anybody on the street. Do you understand? Don't say anything.

Sam, what was the experience you had?

I was sitting parked down in midtown waiting for some- one to come out of a store. A limousine pulled up in front of me and started to back up. It was coming right towards me, so I honked my horn a couple of times to give him a warning, but he just crashed right into me. The fellow got out of the limousine and started screaming and yelling at me. I thought, "My God, I didn't do anything. I ought to yell back at him," but then I thought better of that and I just said, "Oh, excuse me, I'm sorry." He walked off mut- tering and gave me a couple of dirty looks. It was like he had gone insane.

There is a darkness on the Earth at this moment, kids, but it doesn't have to be dark for you. Sam said, "Excuse me." He could have said, "What the heck? I was standing here and you backed into me." There might have been a knife and we might not have him here today. The world has gone crazy, especially New York City. It's all over the world; it's not only here. The hell worlds have been loosed, and if you have anger in you toward anybody, that person can do anything to you. Have you got the idea? Please keep the idea in mind. Just say, "Yes, sir. Yes, sir," to everybody. "Yes, ma'am. Yes, sir." What does it say in the Bible? "Agree with thine adversary lest he rend thee." And they sure can rend you if you're not careful, so watch out.

Doctor, come up here, please. How long do you think it will be before the yellow rain ruins all our crops — before the crops shrivel up and we have no food?

I don't know how long it will be, but I was speaking to someone who is involved in the Department of Environ- mental Protection of our state, a very prominent person. About a year ago, when he got the job as a bureaucrat in this agency, he was very calm. He thought things would be very easy, and he was just going to make some regula- tions. But the last time he had a meeting with one of our groups, he was extremely nervous, extremely upset. He said that now that he's open to all the information that's coming in, he can't believe what is happening. He said, "People are not aware of how serious this thing is." He said there are so many issues to be concerned about, but one of the issues is acid rain. When this stuff comes down, not only does it destroy the paint on our cars, not only does it leave holes in clothes if they're left outside, but it also destroys our crops, which means that food may be scarce in a few years.

Thank you, Doctor. Now I'm going to read a tiny bit of a newspaper article.

What is happening to our world? According to the Marxist theory, environmental problems cannot occur in socialist countries because man and nature are inherently in harmony. Unfortunately, the trees, rivers and air in Eastern Europe do not understand Marx. In Leipzig, once one of the prettiest cities in Germany and now a chemical industry center, neighbors cannot see each others' houses and visitors often vomit after a night of breathing the air.

I wouldn't have any visitors.

In Prague, mothers are advised not to give their babies tap water, even after boiling it. The Czech-East German border is rapidly becoming a huge tree cemetery, the world's best showcase of the effects of acid rain. At the top of some of the mountains, not a single tree survives, just barren landscape with a few remaining stumps. In Cracow, the Polish National Lawyers Association reports that cancer, heart disease and other problems are two to eight times higher than the rest of Poland and the infant mortality rate is more than three times the national average. The 1985 report of the Polish Academy of Scientists noted an appalling increase in the number of retarded school children in upper Silesia, and Poland faces a catastrophic water shortage. Only one percent of the country's water is clean enough to drink, and almost half the water is so polluted that it is unfit for any use. Temporary water shortages now reportedly affect 120 cities and 10,000 small towns. The Academy of Scientists report warned that if the present trend continues, in five years there will be no more water.

I think it's retribution. That's just my feeling; you don't have to feel that way. I feel that the horrors that went on in Europe during the Holocaust are catching up with them. When will the way that we treated the Indians catch up with us? The way we treated the black slaves, when will that catch up with us? It's already catching up with us — our trees are dying. To put it mildly, the one God of all of us is mad, and He's not going to put up with it. There are going to be changes, and you and people like us are going to make the changes — by changing ourselves. Do you understand? You have to keep God in your heart and love in your heart.

This is from another article I read.

New York Times, Moscow, July 25th:

A prominent Russian writer recently produced a tattered old Bible and with a practiced hand turned to Revelations. "Listen," he said, "this is incredible!"

"'And the third Angel sounded and there fell a great star from Heaven, burning as if it were a lamp, and it fell upon the third part of the rivers and upon the fountains of the waters, and the name of this star is called Wormwood. And the third part of the waters became wormwood and many men died of the waters because they were made bitter."

In the dictionary he showed the Ukrainian word for wormwood, "a bitter wild herb used as a tonic in rural Russia, chernobyl."

Chernobyl is the wormwood in the Bible! Do you know what has happened to Europe because of that explosion in Chernobyl? I know because I have people in Germany, I have people in the Netherlands, I have people in Poland. The water is poisoned. They can't use it. I read somewhere that in the end a million people will die because of that bad water that resulted from the nuclear accident at Chernobyl, or wormwood.

Isn't it amazing that the Bible foretold two thousand years ago the things that are happening now? It's just a thrill!

I want to read one little tiny piece from the Bible. It says:

I saw four angels standing on the four corners of the Earth, holding the four winds of the Earth, that the winds should not blow on the Earth, nor on the sea, nor on any tree. And I saw another angel ascending from the East,

> having the seal of the living God: and he cried with a loud
> voice to the four angels to whom it was given to hurt the
> Earth and the sea.[1]

Can you see it? Angels standing in each part of our world, not asking whether we're Jewish or Christian or Hindu or anything, just angels that don't belong to any religion, standing on the four corners of the Earth. I've prayed many nights to those four angels to please hold off. The angel with the seal of God is saying:

> Hurt not the Earth, neither the sea, nor the trees, till we
> have sealed the servants of our God in their foreheads.[2]

What does that mean? To me it means hold off until we get ready. How long? We've had six thousand years now trying to get ready, two thousand years since Jesus' time. We've got to get ready now. The angels are not holding off any longer. They're letting go. Do you follow this? I prayed and prayed for them to hold off, hold off until we got ready, until we got decent, until we got anger out of us, until we got hate out of us, lust out of us, meanness out of us. They're not going to wait any longer, but we can come through with God.

You've got to live differently. We can't live in the sloppy, rotten way we've lived. One of the TV evangelists said that the sixties revolution of sex is over and virginity is in style. We can't live the LSD way. We can't live the heroin way — I don't know the names of drugs, what is it, crack? We can't live that way. We've got to live clean and come through right. I know anyone living clean will come through perfectly. That's not my lecture, but it's what I have to say. That's my stuff to scare you into being good. You know, they used to say, "You'll go to hell." Now I just say, "You'll go into the tribulation, so be good." It's a new style.

The world is a wonderful place. God gave us everything we need here and when He got through, He said, "It is good." That's what it says in Genesis. The world is better than good. It is only people that are the trouble, so let's change the world back to what God intended by changing our little bit — ourselves. We are responsible for our little bit. That is your duty in this life; that is why you came down at this very, very special time, as the changes lead into the millennium. It is a very, very special time, and you all chose to come down. Many people have also chosen to come down in other difficult places like so many of the countries in Africa. They chose to come down to suffer and pay off their karma because this is the time when they will be able to pay a lot of it off.

Tell me, how can I wake you up, kids? Not mentally, for you are awakened mentally, or you wouldn't be here. How can I awaken you deep inside to the fact that within a mere twelve or thirteen years, not one item on the Earth will be the same — not education, not economics, not medicine, nothing will be the same, nothing in the world.

It's hard for you to take in, but when it says in the Bible that you will not be able to buy or sell, think for a moment what that means. It means you won't be able to buy or sell without the mark of the devil. If you refuse to take the mark, what does that mean? Start with gasoline. You won't be able to buy any gasoline. Even if you stole some, you won't be able to get a driver's license. You won't be able to get the little sticker on the front of your car. You won't be able to get any shoes or clothes or food. Have you ever thought about what that means? You won't be able to pay the rent. You won't be able to pay for the telephone — well, I'll be glad when there's no telephone! You won't be able to ride the subways — that's good. You'll have to buy a horse, but maybe they'll put a stamp on the horse and say you can't ride down the road without having a license for the horse. Think out what it means. I thought it out one day and I thought, Wow! It takes in everything! This will last for three and a half years, so for that time you'll have to sit somewhere. I don't know where you'll sit. Maybe underground.

Not a city, nor the contour of the Earth, nor the world, nor the economic system will be the same; not even your bodies will feel the same, nor your mind, nor emotions. Nothing you have ever known will be on Earth. You wonder how can this be? Well, hang around and find out. Because your atoms are going to get spiritualized. The things that you like now, you're not going to like then. I used to adore chocolate. Now I hate it. The shows that you used to like, you won't like to go to see. You'll be bored. What else? Potato chips? Well, I read that if you're under fourteen, potato chips are good for you. That was in one of those tabloids though.

Yes, week after week the Masters and the Intergalactic Council, the Hierarchy, through this body you call Hilda, have been trying to warn you and prepare you. Yes, you mentally understand, but have you awakened to the magnitude of the times in which we live as we go into the Aquarian Age, go into a new way? You go on worrying about the same things: Shall I marry this one or that one? Shall I be homosexual, heterosexual, or maybe not make up my mind and be bisexual? Or shall I be celibate? All these thoughts, and the world's going to pieces. Shall I move? No, I can't — I have a job and security, my child has a good school, I have a lease. Will I pass my exams? Will I graduate? Will I get money to go to school? And so on, ad infinitum. Who cares? Who cares about all that? Jesus said, "What is that to thee? Follow thou Me." What did he mean, follow him? Follow him up into the sky? No — follow his way. What does he teach? Love, truth — the same things Moses taught. Follow my way, my way of love. Jesus spoke of all this in a much better way, more poetically than I, in Luke 17:26-33:

> And as it was in the days of Noah, so shall it be also in the days of the Son of Man. They did eat, they drank, they married wives, they were given in marriage, until the day that Noah entered into the ark, and the flood came, and destroyed them all.

Can't you just see Noah, who was six hundred years old, and the ark door closing, with the rains coming down and the people standing outside who had been making fun of him for the hundred years that it took him to make it? Can't you just see them as the flood comes up on them and the ark goes away? Have some imagination in this.

> Likewise also, as it was in the days of Lot, they did eat, they drank, they bought, they sold, they planted, they builded; but the same day that Lot went out of Sodom it rained fire and brimstone from heaven and destroyed them all.

Do you think these are fairy tales? Nothing doing. It happened.

> Even thus shall it be in the day when the Son of Man is revealed. In that day, he which shall be upon the housetop, and his stuff in the house, let him not come down to take it away; and he that is in the field, let him likewise not return back...Whosoever shall seek to save his life shall lose it; and whosoever shall lose his life shall preserve it.

If you go underground to save your life, you may lose it. You can go underground, that's smart, but you have to have an objective in mind. The objective is this age of wonder that's coming upon us, the Age of God. When you hear "New Age" coming from some political man's mouth, just close your ears because the Antichrist will use the term "New Age" to fool you. I say the Age of God, the Sathya Age. When that comes, you have to die to yourself, and I'll tell you why a little later.

I plead with you, let us start the new life expected of us right now — a life of unconditional love and trust.

Unconditional love is a big phrase and a big thought, but what does it really mean? Think as I talk. It means being reborn from being petty, miserable, worrying Earth creatures, into a peace within, a feeling of completeness. That's what unconditional love is — being reborn from being the petty little people we've always been. Work as one who is ambitious without ambition, without worrying about the outcome or, as Vivekananda says, "Don't worry about the fruits thereof." Just do your work. God is watching you, the Masters are watching you. I say to everyone that the Masters of the Great White Lodge are aware of you. Everyone who takes their teachings seriously — and I repeat this in the name of Count Saint Germaine and Master Hilarion — everyone who takes their teachings seriously is being watched and helped by them in these hard times.

Beloveds, you can't beat this game down here. You can't beat it your own way, particularly at this time, because God has written a script and is now having auditions for those who are to play the parts. So start practicing and rehearsing your parts and be adept at God's way of acting out life. If shouting would wake you up to what is in store for you, I would yell myself hoarse. But you have to open like a rose in the sun, and the sun is love, unconditional love.

At the last meeting, it was a beautiful sight when I saw so many of you courageously and sincerely stand up, not caring what others thought, with tears running down your cheeks as your souls were cleansed by the Holy Spirit that descended from heaven upon us. Those tears were not of remorse — those tears were of the soul. Letters have come to me from so many who told me they were cleansed. The Lord entered their hearts, and they were renewed in spirit. It was an inspiration to them. How many of those who stood up felt that holy light come upon them? How many have felt different since? Put your hands up high. In fact, stand up and give testimony to God Almighty. You feel different, do you? Do you feel cleansed? Thank you. You're giving testimony not to me, but to Him, the One God.

Holy Spirit in ancient Hebrew is *Ruach Ha-Kodesh*. It means breath or wind. So this Holy Spirit is not a recent thing — it was written in Isaiah long ago, and it is in Acts 1-2. We call it the Holy Spirit, the Holy Ghost. It is the breath of God blowing us clean. You should not take it for granted and say merely, "Yes, I feel a cold breeze." It's God blowing on you. The promise.

We should be in awe.

These meetings are so unusual that for new people these things are sometimes hard to understand. I speak from the heart, and only a heart can understand.

I am asked to lecture in so many places, and I refuse because I have worked so hard and long with you people. I want to see you finished and free and written in the Book of Life. It is my heart's desire to see you free. You've come here so faithfully. Make God your goal. Do all the other things you have to do and be grateful for any job you have, but let God be foremost in your mind. Businesses are closing down now — four thousand people in one place out of work, fifteen hundred in another place — so be grateful for any job you have. I don't care what it is — cleaning a house, anything. But make God your goal. "Put a throne in your heart," Sathya Sai Baba says, "and let no one sit in that throne but the Lord."

I have known people with power, but no love. I have known people who can do miracles, but have no love. I have known people who can draw crowds and gather great money for it, but have no love. So they are failures in this life or any life. Saint Paul spoke about unconditional love in a far better way. You're all familiar with 1 Corinthians 13:

> Though I speak with the tongues of men and of angels and have not love, I am become as sounding brass, or a tinkling cymbal. And though I have the gift of prophecy, and understand all mysteries, and all knowledge; and though I have all faith, so that I could remove mountains, and have not love, I am nothing. And though I bestow all my goods to feed the poor, and though I give my body to be burned, and have not love, it profits me nothing. Love suffers long and is kind; love envies not; love vaunts not itself, is not puffed up. Love does not behave itself un-seemly, seeks not her own, is not easily provoked, thinks no evil. Love rejoices not in iniquity, but rejoices in the truth. Love bears all things, believes all things, hopes all things, endures all things. Love never fails; but whether there be prophecies, they shall fail; whether there be tongues, they shall cease; whether there be knowledge, it shall vanish away. For we know in part and we prophesy in part, but when that which is perfect is come, then that

which is in part shall be done away. When I was a child, I
spake as a child, I understood as a child, I thought as a child;
but when I became a man, I put away childish things. For
now we see through a glass, darkly, but then face to face:
now I know in part, but then shall I know even as also I am
known. And now there abides faith, hope and love, these
three, but the greatest of these is love.

Jesus loved. He doesn't belong only to Christians. He belongs to the Jews,
to the Buddhists, to the Hindus, the Muslims, to all who live the way of the
truth of life — love. He is too big, too great to be owned by one group. He
fills the universe. For did he not say, "The Father and I are one," God and I
are one? And for that did he not pay a price, a heavy price, for breaking
down the little barriers of mental separation? He went on the cross willingly
and opened up a great new world for us to enter when we go past our labels,
our little "isms." You have been brainwashed with labels from birth, and
now it is time to think for yourself, from deep in your intuition, about what
truth is.

Jesus left us a gift of freedom, and we are made new by accepting this gift
of the Spirit. It is so simple. We give up our little ego's opinions in exchange
for the great spiritual truths, the truths that have existed in all the ages since
the world was created. We let in the light of truth, and we are free. Know
the truth and it shall set you free from the bondage of your self.

What is that truth? The one and only truth is that we were created perfect
and perfect shall we be.

Your mortality shall take on immortality in this age of Adam, the Adamic
Age. We are all children of Adam and Eve. Do you understand that? Adam
and Eve were in God-consciousness, and they fell because they didn't listen
to God. It's not a matter of their putting a fig leaf on and hiding some part.
That's not what the story is all about. What the story is all about is that they
were in God-consciousness, but they disobeyed God and so fell into self-
consciousness. The result is what we are, and we have suffered ever since
with self-consciousness: What is my real career? Shall I get a better job?
Where will I live? Whom shall I marry? What shall I do? How shall I dress?
We have become self-conscious instead of being conscious in God.

We must come out of that Adamic state, and this is the time to come out
of it. That is what being reborn is. It is time for all of us to be reborn back
into the consciousness of God, back into this great consciousness which is

like a great universe. Let us step over all the pebbles and the dirt and the muck we've put here and walk back into the consciousness of God.

Let's say you're in the consciousness of God, and then you get petty and complain, "That person said this about me." Whew! You're right out again, out of the Garden of Eden. So you say, "Oh no. I'm out again." Nothing doing! Cut! Cut that thought. Cut! And back in you go, into the consciousness of God, and say, "That person must've had a bad time to be so mean. I will send that person unconditional love." It's as simple as that, kids. We have to keep unconditional love all the time. We may fall out of the Garden of Eden, but we have to walk back in fast. As quickly as the negative thought comes, say, "Cut." Go back with a good thought, and you're in the consciousness of God again. You're in attunement and you're in safety, no matter what happens around you. You understand that?

Don't try to struggle to give up the negative things. Let Jesus do it for you. He did it for all of us two thousand years ago, and still we haven't accepted his gift.

As I told you before, Nityananda suffered like mad every time people came near him. He took on their karma until his pain was excruciating. Ramakrishna took on cancer to pay off the debt. All the great saints who have come have done it. Jesus came and went on the cross willingly; nobody put him there. He did it for us years ago, and still we haven't accepted the grace of his sacrifice. Let us accept it here tonight.

I want to talk on love. You can't very well love a God up there that you can't see. The Jewish people are not even allowed to say His name. But you can love down here.

I want to play a song for you, and I want you to think of someone you love so much that you could burst. I want to see love just fill this room. If it's your mother, if it's your father, if it's your grandmother, whoever it is, just love them like you've never loved before. You might have had a lover who walked out on you, and you crushed the rose and said, "That rotten person." Open the rose up again and see how wonderful you felt when you were with that person. Maybe you lost somebody in your family. Try to remember all the good times you had with him or with her, not the bad times and the dying times. If you have a husband who is mean to you, remember the nice times and forget the bad times. If you have a wife who is nagging you, forget the nagging and say, "It does her so much good to get it out of her system." And vice versa. Do you understand? I want you to think on all these things during the music. If it's the ocean you love, love the ocean. If it's the sun you love, love the sun. If it is Mary, then let it be Mary. If it is the Absolute Mother, let it be the Absolute Mother. If it is light, if it is Jesus, if it is Sai Baba, Moses, I don't care whom you love, but I'd rather you meditate on someone down here that you have loved. If it is somebody that you loved and walked out on because you didn't like that the person went into drugs or something, remember the good times as this song goes on, will you please? Let's meditate on this right now. Close your eyes. Let your hearts open.

  Hilda plays "Some Enchanted Evening" by Rodgers and Hammerstein II.

Keep your eyes closed, and with your hearts open down here on Earth, invite God into your heart. Put a throne in your heart and invite the Lord to sit on it. Say, "You're first, Lord, in my life. God, you're first." Feel it right now. Feel the love generated in this room. When I feel the Holy Spirit start to come, I will call you up. Don't come until that time. In a few minutes, I'm going to ask those who wanted to stand up last class for a blessing and couldn't get up the courage, to come forward. When I ask you, you will come just as you are, with all your unworthiness, all your so-called sins, all your dirt, and be cleansed by the *Ruach Ha-Kodesh*, or Breath of God, the Holy Spirit.

Jesus said he would go, but that he would send down the Comforter, the Holy Ghost, to help us through the hard times of the tribulation. It's hard to get rid of our own iniquities, but let's just know that this breath will come soon. I feel it coming already on my hands up here. I feel it beginning to blow through the room. I see the candlelight being blown. Let this breath blow down on us and cleanse us.

Just sit quietly and let your inner Self decide if you will bring yourself, your dirt, to be cleansed and reborn into the consciousness of God. For this Jesus went on the cross and suffered for you and me. Those who feel it within themselves to come up, come down the side aisles and stand quietly in front here until you receive the touch of the Holy Spirit. I'm waiting for the Holy Spirit to come in its full force. We'll sing "Amazing Grace."

> Amazing grace
> How sweet the sound
> That saved a soul like me.
> I once was lost
> But now I'm found

Was blind
But now I see.

Stand for one moment and let the breath of God touch you. I call upon the Holy Spirit to rain upon us. Let us feel You as a cold breeze upon us, a coldness on our skin. Let us know you're here, Masters of Wisdom, let us know you're here. Hierarchy, we are sincere here.

Believe, believe with all your heart that you can be free from all the stupidity of this whole life and all your lives in one second of just saying, "I believe in the truth of God, that I was created perfect and perfect I am and was never different." Within you is that spark of light that has never been touched by dirt, never been touched by the muck of this Earth. Dive into it right now.

Holy Spirit of God, flow down on us. Flow down on us. I'm depending on You. Flow down on us and heal these people.

Let this light flow down on you. Let the golden light flow down on you. Feel an essence of gold flow down on you now. Let the essence of God flow down on you now. Feel that you're being cleansed, that you never will be the same again, that you're renewed and reborn into the consciousness of God, where you belong.

Oh God, God, God, touch these souls here this night. Let us feel Your breeze, my Lord. Let me feel it. Thank You.

It's coming. Put out your hands so you can feel it. Put your hands upward and receive of it. Know that it's God breathing on you, that it can go right through every cell of you, that all you've ever done is forgiven. Those who are sitting down, pray hard for those who are up here. Pray hard.

Shambala. Shambala. Oh God, God, You will never forsake us. Jehovah, Lord of Hosts, did You not say, "Try Me and prove Me"? We try You this night. We believe in the mighty power within us.

Feel the breeze upon you. Those who can feel the breeze, put your hands up and receive of it. It's like a coolness that comes over you.

God, this is a sacred moment. Angels watching us, record each one's name, my angels, each one that stands here and sits here. Record their names into the Book of Life and give them courage to walk in glory. Shambala. Shambala.

Blessed are the meek and lowly for they shall inherit the Earth, and they shall walk upon this Earth in its newness, and the glory shall be upon them and they shall glorify the Father. Blessed art thou.

Thank you for your standing, and thank you for your faith, and thank you for coming here. Just hold the power and let the blessing be upon you. How many felt the coolness of the air? I did up here. Thank you.

One person has gone into samadhi, and I'm going to make him speak from his place. It's not planned. Speak what you hear from the Holy Ones.

This moment is real. The moods and thoughts you think are real at other times are the illusion. This confidence in light and love is real. The fears and worries you have at other times are the illusion. This concept of yourself you have is real. Images of yourself at other times that are not like this are the illusion. The Golden Age you envisioned as the words of that song were sung, that Golden Age is real. The suffering that you think you see will pass. The light and love you feel this moment will last forever. This moment tie a knot, tie a knot in your mind so that you can always come back to this moment in the midst of your moods, your depressions, your fears, and know what is real and what is the illusion. God bless you all.

Who spoke to you?

Sanat Kumara.

Sanat Kumara, Lord of the World.

Go home and hold this. Don't start talking. Don't talk anything except God and God experiences for the next half hour. If somebody comes up and talks something else to you, tell him instead about an experience, a dream. Hold this power. Hold the power, beloveds, because the outside world is going to bang at you after this. It is not going to like this. Do you understand? It's not going to like the light coming into you, so you must hold firm.

Chapter Three

Courage and Mastery

Change will come! The day of awakening is not so far away. When it comes, there will be a revelation of the true power of God, a manifestation of the omnipresence of the Lord. This will be the signal for a great move forward and for the weeding out of those who are not ready to accept the challenge of the moment. It will be just so, mark my words, but few will listen, very few.

After the storm, there will be a new beginning, and the atmosphere will be completely different. It will be a new age, the age of love, of harmony, of cooperation, replacing the age of war and fighting and hatred and jealousy and greed and all those negative aspects of life. Everyone should prepare now — now! — for this change, for I promise you that it will come, and only those who are ready will survive.

I have given you the warning. I have given you my message a thousand times and no one who hears my words can claim ignorance. No one who has come here to these meetings more than three times can claim ignorance of the fact that they have to change, because I'm always yelling about it.

I have a letter I'd like to read to you. It's from someone who has been coming to this class. I just adore it when I hear from her. She says:

> When I came to you four years ago I was a heroin addict
> and a call girl, a nice way of saying prostitute. Thanks to
> your meetings and some help from Alcoholics Anonymous,
> my entire life has been transformed. I brought my mother
> and brother with me tonight. They're new on the path and
> have wanted to hear you for a long time. I thank you for

my life from the bottom of my heart and for these classes,
which have meant so much to me over the years.

Today I work with people with AIDS at Bailey House,
because it could have been me. But for the grace of God, it
could have been me dying from AIDS. This work renews
me and strengthens me on a daily basis. We lost eight
young people this past month. Please pray for their souls
to be at peace.

I thank you again for restoring my soul and leading me
to still waters and the green pastures of the spirit, the soul
and the heart.

Isn't that beautiful?

With your permission, I would like to talk on "Shoah," the documentary
on the Holocaust. For the three days it was on television, I sat there feeling
the city full of anguish. This feeling, the anguish of the Jews watching this
picture, was coming in my windows until it was just terrible. Watching
"Shoah" was worse than seeing the horrible photographs we are so used
to, where we see graves with bodies in them, because it left everything to
your imagination. There were no people in it. It would show a train moving
toward a place and then the narrator talked about it. What we imagined was
even worse than seeing the things we have gotten so hardened about that
we can look at them without being affected.

The thing that got me, until it was clarified in the last ten minutes, was
that the filmmaker kept on making a particular play on showing a cross with
Jesus on it or a church with people outside, Christians talking of how they
saw the Jews taken away. He was making a point about Christians and Jews,
and it was getting heavy. But in the last ten minutes he said, "I feel I have
made a successful picture. It has taken me eleven years," he said, "but I am
in anguish." Because for eleven years he had dwelt on that horror and I
suppose he had some grind against Christianity, whereas it was Hitler, as
we know, who did it, and Hitler had no religion at all.

Because so many letters came in to me about the show, I'm going to talk
on it a little bit tonight. Here's a letter that was sent to me that I would like
the author to read to you.

I've spent some time recently thinking about the Holocaust and my impressions of World War II from having
lived in Europe in the mid-fifties. My father was in the Air

Force and we were stationed in France from 1954 to 1957. The stories I heard as a child were those of ordinary people trying to live under the Nazi tyranny. The merchants in my small village were so afraid that they felt they had no choice but to obey those bullies who invaded their village and dictated the routine of everyone's daily lives.

I know stories secondhand of extensive underground organizations throughout France that fought to subvert the policies of the Nazis. A French woman whose American husband taught in my school told my class of the underground newspaper she helped run in Paris, about people risking their lives to use the typewriters during working hours or after hours, about people secretly running the copying machines, which were very primitive and messy by today's standards, trying to leave no trace of ink on their fingers as they kept France informed of the real news behind the scenes in occupied France.

The story I wish to tell is a tragedy. I heard about it from my parents when they went to visit a war memorial in a picturesque small village near where we lived. There had been some underground activity near this Christian village in central France. Radio messages were believed by the Nazis to have been transmitted from the village, and Resistance forces had destroyed some Nazi encampments in the area. The Nazis believed that the village was the center in a local network of Resistance fighters. What the Nazis did in retaliation was to order the entire village rounded up. As all the young men had been taken away to work camps or had left to work in the Resistance elsewhere, the only ones left in the village were women, children and old men.

The Nazis gathered everyone up and took them to the local Catholic church and proceeded to destroy the entire town. They then set fire to the church with all of the villagers in it. One woman climbed up a very high wall to a stained glass window and threw her baby and then herself out of the window. She climbed down a well near the church and hid with her child. After dark she left the village with her baby, alone. They were the only survivors in the entire village. It was only discovered after the war that the Nazis had destroyed the wrong village, mistaking the spelling of the names of two twin-sister villages.

This story is meant to complement what we are trying to do here with unity among all religions. Peoples from all walks of life and religions suffered at the hands of Hitler's machine. In this country we tend to forget that it was ordinary everyday people who were attempting to stop Hitler from achieving his goal in their country, in their villages. They had to work in small ways and many of them paid the ultimate price with their lives.

It can appear from the distance of time that there was little or no help, but I have heard too many stories of churches, schools and people helping to hide the persecuted. I have more than once asked myself if I would be able to be as courageous as these people in caring for my brothers and sisters in such times of need. I believe that everybody should take a moment and say, "Yes, I would take that chance for one person to get through some future holocaust. I might take someone's hand and hide him from someone or protect her in her time of need."

These early experiences have helped to shape my search for real protection in such times of crisis so as not to have to rely on money, objects or other people for my sense of security. I've always been haunted by an urgency to prepare for a future horror to come that will be ten times worse than the last and from which, as the Bible says, "No man will survive, save these days are shortened." And I believe they have been. I believe they are being shortened so that we can survive.

The Holocaust is now. In Cambodia they shot everybody who had glasses on and anybody with an education. That's our modern Holocaust. By the grace of these classes I have seen that these days will be shortened and that with a single-minded faith in God we can come through this pending tribulation and create the Sathya Age. Thank you.

Here is another letter that was sent to me.

Dear Hilda,

My father was among those who watched "Shoah" and was deeply affected. He does not want to let go of the past and his pain and fear of Gentile people, especially the Polish people.

It was letters like this that I got from Jewish people that made me decide to talk a little bit about this today, because I felt that "Shoah" did not show the courage of the Jews. It didn't show the heart of the Jews. It didn't show, what should I say, the heroic martyrdom of the Jews that is so real to me. In "Shoah" they were portrayed as downtrodden, with no spirit, but believe me, they had spirit. Believe me, they were courageous.

I want to read from *Hasidic Tales of the Holocaust,*[1] which I think is one of the most wonderful books I've ever read. If you're ever downhearted, read that book. It gives you some guts. In every story, somebody comes through. The positive person comes through — sometimes only one in a whole city — but when they come through, it leaves you high. I want to read you two very short stories about two cousins which show the courage of the Jewish people that I missed in that documentary.

It was a sunny, bright spring day, April 14, 1945, in a camp near the town of Gardelegen. Liberation was close. The Red Army was racing from the east toward the Elbe river and armored divisions of the American Army were advancing toward the river from the west. The Nazis and their collaborators were running out of time and searched for a quick way of killing the slave laborers. Under the direction of a Wehrmacht soldier, young German boys in S.S. uniforms rounded up 1,100 inmates of various nationalities, including one American, herded them into a huge brick hay barn lined with gasoline-soaked straw, and set it afire. Among the human beings in the burning inferno were the two young cousins.

The screams and prayers in the barn were difficult to describe. As the smoke grew more intense and the leaping flames grew higher, screams subsided and were drowned by the sounds of coughing. But the prayers did not stop. All the individual prayers, all the glimmers of hope, united in one phrase — the cry of men, in a babel of languages: "Oh, God, save us!" "Sh'ma Yisroel!" "Hear O Israel, The Lord our God, the Lord is One!" With each wave of engulfing flames, the screams of the burning men became more distant and faint. Suddenly the skies turned black. Thunder shook heaven and earth. The rains came down in streams like a flood.

The flames went out. A handful of young people made their way out of the barn and threw themselves on the flooded ground. The young cousins had won another round with death.

When the rains stopped, the survivors from the burning barn, other inmates, and POWs were loaded on trucks and guarded by Germans and gendarmes, and driven to the woods to be shot.

The woods were a few kilometers from camp. The air smelled fresh and clean. The young brother and his cousin were on one of the trucks.

"I am bored," said one of the guards. "Hey you, Jew boy, sing for me one of your church songs and hymns!" The cousin, a young Hasid, had a very beautiful voice.

It was April 15, 1945, only five days after the holiday of Passover. The young lad started to sing a song from the Passover Haggadah. The melody was a beautiful one. Soon the other slave laborers of various nationalities and the guards joined in the singing. The gentle spring wind carried the song to the other trucks in the death convoy and they, too, hummed the melody.

As they approached the forest, the German guard stopped the singing. "Tell me the meaning of your song; translate it for me." The Hasidic lad translated: "And this it is which has succored our ancestors and us. For it was not one alone who rose against us to annihilate us, but in every generation there are those who rise against us to annihilate us. But the Holy One, blessed be He, ever saves us from their hand."

Imagine them singing that on the way to be shot. You can't tell me that there wasn't courage there, that there weren't heroic people.

When the boy concluded the translation, the German burst into a wild, mocking laughter. "Let's see how your God will save you from my hands."

"I am still alive, but I am not afraid to die," replied the lad.

They reached a clearing in the forest. In groups of six, they were taken to a ravine in the forest and shot. The two cousins were among the last group. On the face of the German guard was an expression of triumph as the young lads were led to their death.

Suddenly, a motorcycle arrived with two high-ranking German officials. They ordered all remaining prisoners to be taken back to camp. Gardelegen had just surrendered to the American Army.

"Call it fate, call it a miracle, call it anything you want," said Mrs. Glatt as she concluded the story about her brother and cousin. "But one thing is clear. We, the Jewish people, with our abundance of faith, will somehow manage to survive forever."[2]

That was the spirit that I didn't feel in that documentary that went on for hours and hours and hours. The filmmaker himself had been hiding in some Christian village and he didn't know the courage of his own people. That's why I brought this up tonight.

I would like you now to sing and to once more do the work we have done for ten years — harmonizing all religions. We'll sing two songs. Let's counteract all that anger and pray for every soul that died there. If they haven't gone up to their heaven yet, let them rise, every one, and be released. We ask pardon for the heresy, that an insane man could rule a country and do such a thing. But when the Antichrist comes, God help us. It won't be only a country he rules, but a world — for a short time, thank God, only for three and a half years, according to the Book of Revelation in the Bible. And we'll come through it with intelligence.

I want one of the softest and holiest of Jewish prayers to be sung this moment for everyone who died in the Holocaust, for they found a heaven.

Sh'ma Yisroel Adonai Elohenu Adonai Echad

(Hear, O Israel, the Lord our God, the Lord is One.)

Now let us sing, "Silent Night, Holy Night" to unite us and not separate us all.

> Silent night, holy night,
> All is calm, all is bright;
> Round yon Virgin, Mother and Child,
> Holy infant, so tender and mild,
> Sleep in heavenly peace, Sleep in heavenly peace.

I promised in the last few meetings that I would help you with your inner struggles so you may be free in the midst of the chaos down here on Earth. We've got to be Masters. We've got to be free from being shoved this way and that way with our minds. Isn't it about time? The world out there is getting a little heavy, so we've got to get stronger. We've got to keep a balance within ourselves.

I often speak of Masters, and perhaps the term bewilders some. Does it bewilder you? Is somebody going to take a whip and master you, make you do something? With me the Masters always sign themselves when they're writing as "Your Elder Brothers," meaning those who have made it to the top. "Master" is the title that was given by the disciples to Jesus. It means one who has mastered the world with all its tests.

Every day you're getting tests, aren't you? And aren't they getting a little stronger every day? That means you're getting better then, if you're getting stronger tests. It means the Masters are saying, "Well, let's give them one a little harder and see what they can do." If you can really feel that the Masters are looking over you and watching you, you're not going to fail. We have to keep a little bit of ego, enough to take us up the path. If you lose all your ego too soon, you become just a flop. What does God say? He spews out of His mouth the lukewarm.[3] We don't want to be spewed out of God's mouth; we want to be strong people. So, believe that you are being watched over. When somebody screams at you and you want to scream back at them, say, "Oh, is that a nice way to speak? Is that a nice way to speak to your Hilda?" This guy called on the phone and he used every word possible. I learned more words — I took a pencil and wrote them down. You wouldn't believe the words he used. And he hung up in my ear with a bang. I waited a minute and I called back and said, "Is that the way to speak to your Hilda?" And he was meek as a lamb. Do you understand? You have to take it on the chin, and sometimes you have to give it.

A Master is one who has mastered the world with its tests. That's all you've got to do. Down here it's a school. This is not the real place, kids. Wait until you get up there. It's amazing, but you can't go too soon. When you go to school, you pay your tuition and you've got to go through with it until you get your degree.

Master does not mean one who holds a whip over us to master us, but rather one who with love encourages us to also master the tests of the world and graduate from this kindergarten. I hope that clears up any erroneous ideas. They are just men and women made perfect, perfected beings who gave up their heavens to stay close enough to us down here to be able to contact us through our own inner faculties, our intuition, to spur us on. You take one step toward them, and they will take ten steps toward you. Did you hear that? You take one step toward them and say, "I'm going to do this."

I'm going to show you the inertia you have. We're going to say, "I'm going to stand up." And then you say to yourself, "No, I don't think I will. Too hot. We just sat down. They'll probably make us sing again." Then say to yourself, "Yes, I am going to stand up" and do it. That's what you call mastery — mastering your senses. You say, "I think I'll go and open that window," and then you think, "Oh, heck, I'd just as soon be hot over here than walk over and open that window." But then say to yourself, "No, I won't think that! I will go over and open that window!" You will be an absolute master.

When so many of you stood up for a blessing at the last two classes, you gave up your past. You felt the blessing of the Holy Spirit, the *Ruach Ha-Kodesh*, the Breath of God, but the negative forces will try to bring back memories of your past. You stood up and you cried. I've never seen so many people crying in my life. It was beautiful. Many of you told me that you were redeemed, that you felt ashamed of your life and it was all going out in these tears. But what comes in? As soon as you get out the door, the negative will come in to you and say something else: "You are not free. Jesus did not free you on the cross. That's a bunch of bunk." As soon as you say, "I'm feeling mean this moment," you open a little avenue above your head and the little imps up there say, "Oh, you're mean, you're mean, you're mean. You're no good, you're rotten, you're not saved, you're not any-thing." It comes on you and on you and on you. You have to hold to the truth; you have to say, "Shut up, up there! I'm sticking to my idea. I'm okay!" Do you understand this?

Someone wrote to me in a letter that as soon as she got home the negative started coming. So she just shouted at it and it stopped. Don't listen to that negative that comes on you and tells you you're no good. Remember, if something comes and tells you you're in the image and likeness of God, you can accept that, but don't accept all that negation that you have made a habit of for so many years, the habit of downing yourself: "I did this, I did that. Fifteen years ago I did that, five years ago I did that, last night I did this, two minutes ago I did this." And so you go on pestering yourself, but no Master would do that. That is why you must build up a formidable will to tell the devil to back off, to say, "Back off! Back off! Back off!" The devil has a yellow spine. It's love that will overcome it. If this negative force comes, take three breaths of love into your heart and breathe it out all around you. Then you do it again. I tell you, the negative will run. You will hear it go screaming off. It will run. The negative can't stand love. Dark can't stand light. That's all you have to do.

When I was going through my initiation with the Masters, they sent me into the inner plane. I was in there and there were these little evil forces coming at me, so I took a bottle and started chasing them with it, just like the thugs on the street do. They didn't care a hang. I came into my body again, and I was soaking wet. The Master standing in my room said, "Go in again!" I had to go in and face that negative again. I went in again. Do you know what I mean by going in? Going into like a dream world. I went in, and this time I caught on. I just stood there with my chest out. I stood there, and those little demons were there, and I breathed love three times in and out of my heart. They ran so fast and disappeared. I came out and the Master said, "Well done." You can't beat evil with evil. You have to beat evil with love.

That is why you must build up a formidable will-power. You must learn patience. You must learn to be free from worry. If worry comes into you, say, "I'll worry about that tomorrow." Irritability will come in. Have you felt irritability in the air lately? In the sunshine? You'll find it in the sunshine because of the break in the ozone. Don't go out in the sunshine without putting strong sunscreen on, because you'll feel irritability out there.

And there's judgment of others. You've got to stop judging others, because that makes gossip. The Masters used to say, "Don't look over the fence into somebody else's garden for weeds. You've got enough weeds of your own to pluck, Hilda." Why look at somebody else's weeds and judge them and look and see what they're like? If you think on them, you'll come down to their level. If you say, "He's no good, he gossips and everything," you immediately have come down to that level.

Stop worrying — it is the burden you borrow from tomorrow. If you're worrying about something that is going to happen tomorrow, I'll tell you what I've learned: all the things I worried about in this life never came to pass. If I could start over, I wouldn't worry, because none of them came to pass. None. Unnecessary extra baggage they were. If you went on a train, you wouldn't put your suitcases on top of you, would you? Where do you put your suitcases on a train? Under the seat, down beside you. So let God carry your luggage, let the train carry it, let Jesus carry it, let Moses carry it. Let God carry your luggage. Didn't Jesus say, "Come unto me, the heavily laden"? Well, let's take him at his word, shall we? Say, "Hey, Jesus, I'm heavily laden. I've got a lot of baggage. Would you help me carry this? Tomorrow I've got a big problem, would you help me carry this luggage tomorrow?" Let's be free and remember to remain free in Christ and let him not have suffered in vain on the cross.

Let us go back a little in time, shall we, just for fun? Close your eyes. What were your ideals at seven years of age? To get a hamburger? What were your ideals then? Did you have any?

What were your ideals, or what did you believe in, at twelve years of age? You must have believed in something. I believed in peace. What did you believe in? Come on, go back. You must have had ideals deep inside, when you weren't playing kick-the-can and hide-and-seek. Fairness — one person says her ideal was fairness. Somebody else yell out. Unity — who said that? At twelve years of age? Pretty good. We've got a saint with us. Anybody else have any ideals at twelve? Security.

At fifteen what were your ideals? This person says she wanted to be in a place where everybody could love each other. Well, here you've got it, here at last. It took a long time, didn't it? All right, what other ideals did you have at fifteen? To finish school so you could be yourself. Couldn't you be yourself while you were at school? You couldn't? Pretty hard, I know. Another person says to sing.

All right, let's go up a little bit. At twenty-two years of age, what were your ideals? To be free. To be free of what? Somebody wanted self-realization at twenty-two. Pretty good. Help change the world to be better. I've got a good crowd here. To end the war. All right.

Now, close your eyes. When did you compromise and feel weighed down? When did you compromise with the ideals that you had when you came out of that womb, when you came down from your star with something to do on this Earth? I know one little boy only two years of age who saw a picture of a UFO. Since then he puts his hat and coat on every day and goes out, saying he's waiting for the star car to come and take him back home again.

When did you start to compromise? Now go back to that time and wipe it out this moment. Take an eraser and wipe out the compromise. Do you feel life has cheated you of your dreams? Put your hands up high if you feel life has cheated you of your dreams. It makes my heart feel sad to see your hands.

Start right now, my beloveds, right this moment to live. I feel like I want to cry, seeing hands up that you've been cheated. You haven't been cheated, because you're still living and there's still time to be yourself. If you don't like what you do, your work, or whatever you're doing, then like it. Make the best of it. Go down as an emissary of God to your work. Go down as an emissary of God as you walk the streets, on the subway, anywhere. Leave a light behind you as you walk down the street. If you sit in a chair, then don't leave some grumpiness there so that somebody else comes and sits down and feels grumpy. Do you understand that one? Leave a light in the seat you sit in, and when you get off the subway, somebody's going to come and sit in it who is down-hearted and they will feel your light lifting them. Be a light in this world.

Do you want to sing your crazy song, "Row, Row, Row Your Boat"? But not "down the stream," instead "gently *up* the stream." Come on, let's sing it.

> Row, row, row your boat,
> Gently up the stream.
> Merrily, merrily, merrily, merrily,
> Life is but a dream.

What are you making such a big fuss about life for? Wake up from your dream. That's your theme for this week. Life is but a dream. When somebody comes at you and life gets terrible and the subway's full and there are no seats and the boss wants to fire you, just say to yourself, "Life is but a dream," and don't worry.

I got a call from a person who said she had just lost her house and all these things were happening to her. I said, "For God's sake, why don't you go out and find another place? Maybe around the corner is just some wonderful thing waiting for you. You've been kicked out of this house so you could get into another one." She called back the next day and said she found a wonderful place, and life was wonderful. It had changed. We're afraid to change. We're afraid of everything — afraid to change our house, afraid to change this, afraid to change that. Do you understand? Let life open for us.

You have never been truly young. You have been burdened since you were born. You took one look at the world and someone immediately hit you and you started to cry. Bang on the behind! Isn't that a rotten way to come into this life? You're up there. You say to the Masters, "I'm going down to do good works down there," and as soon as you come out of that womb, they hit you. And you say, "It's started already. What kind of a place is this? They told me up there I was going to go down to a nice school called Earth, and as soon as I arrive they start hitting me, beating me up."

Now learn to be young and free. Learn to laugh, learn to be free. Everybody, learn to be young. Don't smother yourself with opinions. You're smothered with opinions. Don't smother yourself with sickness, with sickness thoughts and fears. You see a pimple and you say, "Oh, my God, I've got it," instead of saying, "I am perfect in God and perfect I shall be" — and then you look and it's gone. Flow, flow and laugh in the ethers. Fly in the sky with me and be free! Be free! Call into the ethers the glory of God and dance through life, the dance of life.

Close your eyes this moment. I want you to love somebody with all your heart. Love somebody with all your heart. Think of someone you love or have loved in the past. Visualize them. See them standing in front of you in every detail. Gently breathe this love in and out of your heart center. Somebody you loved so much — it might have been your mother, your father, a lover. It might have been someone who turned on you later, but forget that. Breathe in and out, and send a wave of love, a wave of life to them.

Now say to yourself, "What do I feel when I feel love?" Describe it to yourself. "I feel nice, I feel peaceful, I feel sweet, I feel kind and I can forgive everybody, I can smile at everybody." Go on telling yourself what it feels like to be in love. Now experience it to its fullest — become love and let it fill you and let it flow through you. Feel it going into your legs like a golden substance, into your face, into your hands, into your eyes, into every part of you.

Now fill the room with love. Fill it with love. Let me feel it. Breathe it in and out. Come on now, don't forget to love. Now love somebody else. O love! I'm beginning to feel it. You're not doing it well enough — I haven't felt it enough yet. Come on. Now I'm beginning to feel it. Oh, feel sweet. Let your face look sweet and let your lips turn up. Make yourself so beautiful beyond words that if your Master looks down on you this moment, he will say, "What a disciple I have!" Oh! You look so lovely! You're looking so beautiful now.

With this preparation, listen quietly, with a heart full of love and a head prepared to listen, to these few words before we close. These are sacred words.

Dost thou not know that the Father, who created thee,
dost take care of thee?

Your body, your health — accept His blessings and get well this moment. If your mind is in discord, let Him take your mind also. If your reputation is bad, let Him take your reputation. Everything the Lord takes care of!

Too long hast thou suffered alone. I will take up my
bahka...

That's His shield.

...and my sword and guard thee from now unto eternity.
Thou shalt never again stand alone. Your every need shall
be attended to. Your every thought shall be heard — and
answered. For your crying out in the night has been heard.

Don't move your hand. Don't move an inch. Accept, accept.

Fear not, Children of Light, Children of the Christ Light.
I, the King of Heaven, have taken up your fight. All is well.
Have faith.

It is signed "Lord of the World".

Let the Holy Spirit flow down upon us now. Let us feel this Holy Spirit. I ask that the Holy Spirit come upon us this moment and flow down on us. O Spirit of God, Breath of God, flow down on us. Flow into our hearts, into our bodies, into our minds and into every cell in us and make us your own.

Too long have we waited to come back to you, Lord. Our hearts have been heavy. Our souls have cried. Oh, my Lord, come soon, come soon! We cannot wait much longer. We need Thee upon this Earth, my Lord! My Lord, come soon! Send down Your Comforter this moment and blow on us! I can feel the wind blowing on us. Take of it into your souls. Take of it.

Now let us send out that light to the world. This is for the people you have in mind — call out their names and a stream of light with their names will go up and the angels will grab it and bring blessings to them. Here we go. Yell their names out. Ommm.

Miracles, God, we want miracles. I believe in miracles.

Believe in a miracle.

Chapter Four

Live to Your Highest

I am going to speak tonight about tenacity of thinking. Let's begin with a good prayer. You can say it with me. It goes like this: "Good morning, God. What are You up to today? I want to be a part of it. Thank You." How's that? We want to be a part of it, don't we? We are a part of it.

I asked you not to bring visitors tonight because many people have asked me to tell some of my old stories about myself, and I don't like to do it in front of strangers. If you're new here tonight, don't think I'm telling these stories because I have a big ego. It's because I was asked to do it.

All I can say is that my life has been absolutely wonderful, full of unfolding mysteries. It has been a veritable treasure house. I thank You, God, for making it so wonderful. Without You, God, it would have been dry and barren.

The struggles of the past, the hardships, the disillusionments, the joys, the bliss supreme, all have faded into nothingness. It seems inconsequential to speak of these stories to you. I have always felt it was too trivial to talk about, but the Masters have reminded me that there are those of you going through these same experiences that I once went through. Perhaps to share, as I have been asked to do by many, may brighten the way for someone else and take fear out of you.

We're all linked together, climbing the mountain terrain up to Truth. I signed a contract with the Masters, the Hierarchy, to come down to Earth at the right time. I have often thought how smart they were to know just when to send me down. Why? Because coming down when I did, I had time to do everything, everything I wanted. I had a career in classical dancing, I went overseas to India, met the gurus, wrote and traveled around, and came back in time to find you.

Some of you waited too long to come down. You came down at a hard time. There may be no time for careers, there's no time for doing all the things you would like to do. I had the chance to do them all because I didn't wait up there too long. I came on down and you dilly-dallied in that nice place up there. You said, "I don't want to go down there. I think I'll wait a while, wait a few years." You waited and you waited and you waited and you came down now. Of all the dopey times to come down — that's all I can say — especially when some people tell us that the three days of darkness are coming soon. I don't say they will, because people are always saying something, but people did say it anyway. That wouldn't give you much time to get a record out, get it into the market, and become a Madonna. Right?

All of the hardships have faded into nothingness for me, and the fun of this life is like a bright sun shining. I am glad I came down when I did. I don't regret it. I will share with you tonight a few of my experiences and of my adventures with God.

First of all, I was born into an agnostic family. Now, agnostics are different from atheists. When an atheist looks at a giraffe, he stands there and says, "There ain't no such animal." You understand? That was supposed to be funny. Whereas an agnostic will say, "My mind is open. Just show me. I'm willing to find out." I looked for answers and found them. As the song says, "It's not that I have something that others cannot find. I looked harder and God pulled the strings that held my heart entwined." It's not that one person has something the others don't have. Everybody has the same thing.

I did look hard and I did struggle. I sent my mother to the brink until she joined the spiritual search. I struggled so hard. I'd walk right in from teaching dancing and I wouldn't even say, "Good evening, Mother." I'd walk right upstairs, cross my legs, and start to meditate. This made my mother berserk. Then she started in, and she sent me berserk. I would say to her, "Mother, don't do that! You'll have to incarnate again!" She'd say, "Well, I kind of like it down here." I'd say, "Oh, Mother, don't say that!" I was a real nut. But you have to be whole-hearted, whole-hog, you could say, one-pointed to make it. You don't make it half-way. With one foot on Mammon and one foot on God, you don't make it. It has to be the razor's edge. When your back is against the wall, you darn well make it. And I'm telling you, kids, with all that's coming we have our backs to the wall.

Actually, my mother was ahead of me. We had a large police dog named Blue who loved everyone in our neighborhood. Everybody thought that he belonged to them. If you took him down the street, someone would say, "Blue dog, where have you been? You haven't been home for a long time." Well, once when he was supposedly lost, a lady who was holding esoteric classes brought him back and ended up asking Mother to join her classes in the study of the Bhagavad Gita.

When God wants you to get busy with His work, He finds you and draws you to Him, even if it is through a wayward dog. He uses all ruses to get you when He wants you. You can think back on how He got you. There is a moment of decision in our lives that changes our course. Can you remember when God decided to get you? Can you remember that moment of decision? Mine came when a visiting teacher, who was at the Bhagavad Gita class Mother attended, came to give a class at our house. Mother said, "This holy person is coming tonight. Would you please come?" So I went. He looked at me and said, "Sit down on the floor." I sat. I saw him talking to this one and talking to that one. I thought, "Gosh, what a rotten way to live." Look at me now! I said, "Do you really like doing this?" He gave me a stern look and said, "Shut up."

There was no questioning this teacher. He said, "Sit in lotus position." I didn't know what that was, so he dragged one foot over here and one foot over there. Now, if you've never sat in that position and somebody drags one foot over here and the other over there — a real lotus position, you understand — and says, "Sit there until I tell you that you can move" — well, I never felt such pain in my life, such excruciating agony. I sat there for two hours, but I didn't want to move. I didn't dare move. I don't know whether it was my ego or whether it was his dogmatism. I don't know what it was. Maybe it was some memory bank in me of having sat on the Ganges in that stupid position.

While I was still in that position, he asked me — and that was a good time to ask me, too, while I was in such pain — "Will you give an hour a day to peace?" It was the turning point. I thought for a while because I thought there was some catch to it. He gave me a stern look and asked again, "Will you give one hour for peace a day? Take a vow?" I knew there was something behind it. It wouldn't make life easy for me. There was going to be a change if I said "yes," and I was really scared. Would I give an hour for peace? I felt I was tying myself. I knew it would change the course of my life, and I liked my life. I was a dancer and I liked it. But after much thought and the excruciating pain and wanting to get out of that position, I said, "Yes! I will do it!" What was the changing point in your life? All of you, think inside about when the changing point came. How did you happen to get here to this class, where you sit in this hot place and put up with it and suffer? Who brought you? How did you hear about it? You have to think. Was it by chance, or were the Masters looking over you and seeing a light over your head and saying, "It's time we did something about that one. Let's send him to that hot place and see if he can stand it."

Then they put something into your mind. You might have been in a nice church and you felt, "This is not enough for me, this sitting down and standing up and sitting down and singing a hymn and then standing up again. I want to know a little more about myself."

I suppose everybody has gone to some kind of a psychic, right? When I was in high school, somebody said, "Let's go to a psychic." I didn't know what a psychic was, so of course I went along. The psychic said, "The mother of somebody here will die sitting in a chair." Gosh! Until Mother died, I always thought it was my mother who was going to sit in a chair and die — do you understand what sappy things we are? — instead of saying, "That's not for me. That's a bunch of hogwash!"

Then they took me to a theosophist. We were having a party one night when a person said, "We want to go to a Theosophical Society meeting." So they took me along. I didn't know what the Sam Hill the speaker was talking about and, to tell the truth, I don't know if there could have been in this world a person dumber than I was. The speaker must have been all of thirty. To me she looked about 105, because I was young. I wondered why she wore her hair long like mine when she was so old. Meanwhile, something was going on inside. Why was I being taken to these places? The Masters up there said, "She's a hard nut. Let her turn to two or three hard places to get her cracked open."

Look and see how your life has changed since you've changed. My main impetus in going ahead was a focus on the heavens, or the spiritual, rather than on the material. Now this is what I want to tell you: if you want to make it to God, stop thinking about the material. We have to stop worrying about AIDS and start hoping and praying for a cure. Do you understand the difference? If somebody dies of AIDS, should we cover them with more darkness? Or should we send them on into the Light? We've got to turn about, completely change our attitude towards life. Stop thinking of the material, and make everything in the material into the spiritual.

So back then, I just turned myself around and wouldn't think of anything material. I did my work, yes, I taught dancing, but I floated around when I taught dancing. I don't think they learned many ballet positions, but they sure got God. We floated around. Later, when somebody took over my class, a ballet person, she asked, "What did Hilda teach them?" A lady said, "Well, she taught them more than you're going to teach them. She taught them how to live. She taught them about the light within them." You understand?

I made everything wonderful. I refused mentally to have anything to do with the lower thoughts and feelings of the world. I passed up gossip and shut up. If you want to gossip about something, gossip about yourself, and let others go out and tell everyone how rotten you are. You'll stop your gossip pretty quickly. Why gossip about somebody else? They're already down or else you wouldn't be gossiping about them. Haven't they got enough problems without you adding to them? So gossip about yourself, not about others. Well, anyway, I wouldn't gossip.

I lived in the positive. I was young. I hadn't gone to India yet. I was still in my mother's house.

Now, this is a must for all of you: disregard the negative, and love and live in the thoughts of God. Turn everything into God. Here's an example. Somebody told me that someone said to them, "If you go on like this, you're not going to make it." I said, "Gee, that was a wonderful thing that person said to you." He said, "Well, I didn't think so." I told him I would have said to myself, "Wow, I'll try harder then, and I will make it." Do you follow me?

Kids, you have to change. There's not much time. If the three days of darkness are coming, you have to hurry and start changing. Stop gossiping. Stop being anything you are down here and start living up there. It doesn't mean you have to be a fool. You still go to work, but work becomes a pleasure because you're doing it for the Lord. You're doing it for Krishna. You're doing it for Jesus, for Moses, for anybody you want to be doing it for. Make your work a different experience. I sold postcards for one week. That's all the work I could find when I was in high school. I took such an interest in what I was doing, and I sold about one postcard a day because I wanted to get the right one for the person. "Who is it for? Your mother? Oh, let me help you." I'd go through dozens of postcards to find the right one for the person's mother. I took such an interest that they fired me.

That reminds me of the time I took a typing job and couldn't type. I went down to the Y and somebody was typing. I said, "How do you type? I'm starting a job tomorrow." She said, "Just concentrate and keep a rhythm." So if you want to type, that's your answer. You don't need to go to any school. You've already learned it: concentrate and keep a rhythm. Well, it's pretty hard to keep a rhythm when there are no letters marked on the keys of the typewriter. It was a blank one with no A-B-C. The others were doing about 105 cards a day and I was doing five. The supervisor came up to me and asked, "Miss Charlton, how many cards are you doing a day?" The Masters had told me that I had to tell the truth about everything, so I looked him in the eye and I said, "Five." He reeled over backwards and said, "We don't mind about quantity. All we want is quality." If only you could have seen the quality, the erasures! But you know, if you tell the truth, something happens. The other person can't blast you. It's a very funny thing. It's a strange, strange thing about telling the truth.

I used to read dance books. I read all the autobiographies of anybody who made it, a singer, a dancer, anyone who made it through difficulties. I thought, "If they can do it, I can do it. If they can do it, I can do it. If they can do it, I can do it. I can make it to God if they can make it to singing." Do you understand? It takes the same energy to do everything. They all had one characteristic in common, all those people in all those books and Paramahansa Yogananda in his book — a determination to succeed by placing their energy on the chosen path and not diverting it off onto many, many avenues.

I want to tell you one thing. If the Masters or the Hierarchy — if it is really the Hierarchy speaking, and you have tested in the name of Christ three times[1] — if they tell you what to do, they will make it possible for you to do it. I had to move out of my mother's house because my brother was making life a little on the miserable side. I had come into God, and he was still agnostic. I didn't want to move, because he didn't make me miserable; he was just making himself miserable.

I moved to a studio in a building where everybody went home at night, and I was there all by myself with a flimsy door. It was miserable, very scary. I used to be really afraid. I'd lay there and I'd say, "God, I'd rather die than be a coward. I'll stay here." Then the Masters said, "Move from this place." Immediately somebody came and said, "There's a little neighborhood bank that's vacant that you can have for thirty-five dollars a month."

You see, the Masters made it possible. If they tell you to do a thing, they will also make it possible for you to do it. If the Masters say change your job, then the job will come up that they want you to do. Do you remember in Yogananda's autobiography when they sent Lahiri[2] way up into the mountains because they wanted him to meet Babaji, and when he was through, they brought him down into town again? They know how to fiddle you around.

Years ago, downtown at the classes at Saint Luke's where we were so crowded together, I saw somebody walking off the stage one day. I was a dub. I used to have students sit on the stage, and I would sit down below. Very humble, you know. I had just come back from India. Now I'm not so humble. I've got a little more brains now. So I saw this person walk out, and I said to the Masters, "Gee, I'm a rotten teacher, that person walked out." They said, "Daughter, don't you understand? She is pregnant. It was too hot for her. We put it into her mind that she left the electricity on, and she went home to turn it off." The Masters had put that thought in her mind to get her out of the heat. Do you see how they take care of you?

Along this line, to get back to these old stories, one day the Masters said, "Go into town." I was living on a mountaintop in Santa Barbara by then, about ten miles up a very steep and winding road. I went to Bea, with whom I was living, and I said, "I'm going down into town." I had no money because I thought it said in the Bible, "You have to go without: you have to go on the highways and the byways." I've never found it in the Bible since then. I've quoted it a million times, but I looked it up the other day, and there's nothing in the Bible that says the highways and the byways. Anyway, I thought that's what it said, so I obeyed it and I had no money. Bea asked, "How are you going?" I said, "I don't know. The Masters said I must go." She asked, "Well, where are you going?" I said, "I don't know. They haven't told me where I'm going."

So I rode down with her husband and all at once I gave orders without thought, "Please, Skip, take me to the post office." I walked into the post office, and the wife of Rod White, the violinist, came running up. She said, "Oh, Hilda! I've been looking for you. Come to my house. I've been wanting you. I need you so much." The Masters knew who needed me, and they knew where to send me, too. It was a very disruptive house, noisy and everything that I didn't need at that time, or felt I didn't need. I felt I needed quiet, meditation, eyes closed, breathing in and breathing out, but that's not what the Masters said. They wanted to send me into a lousy, noisy place where I'd get strong. Kids running around, dogs barking and biting — oh, what a place! The Masters knew better. You think you know what you need, but the Masters know what you need better than you know because they can look into your inner Self.

Don't have fear on this path. Trust it. Sometimes a trembling will come in your body. Have you had that trembling? It's almost as if a body inside your body is trembling. Or all at once you'll feel as though an insect has bitten you while you're in meditation. Now what that is, is the opening of new nerve centers for your new body. That feeling of something biting you is really the opening up of something. The trembling is a quickening of your body into this New Age of God — it's a new kind of body, your new God body. If you're not getting the trembling, don't worry and think you're lost. You aren't. If you do get it, don't worry.

I used to lie down and say, "Oh, Shiva, stop dancing in me, will you?" It seemed like every little atom was dancing separately. I went to a yogi and I just started to say, "You know..." I didn't have to say any more. He said, "That's all right. Keep it three days, and I'll take it away." He let me have the shaking for three days; then he took it away. It's the awakening of our bodies. We're going into a new type of body now.

I would like to tell you another story because it's a very vital one. When my father passed on, my mother said, "Oh, please don't leave. Stay with me, Hilda." I kept saying, "My mother is holding me, my mother is holding me, my mother won't let me go, my mother is holding on to me." All day long I'd think, my mother is holding me. I can't go out into the world; I can't go out and do my work. My mother's holding me; my mother's holding me. All at once the Master came to me and said, "Your mother is not holding you. You are holding your mother!" Being fresh and smart-alecky and young, I, of course, said, "What do you mean, I am holding my mother? That's crazy!"

Then it dawned on me. I was covering my mother with thought forms, and she was acting out what I was feeding into her mind. Do you understand that? It is very important you understand because often, when you are gossiping, when you are thinking of someone, you are putting a haze, a grey cloud, around them, feeding it into their computer, and then they act it back to you. I had put a gray cloud around my mother, which said, "Hilda shouldn't go, Hilda shouldn't go, Hilda shouldn't go." As soon as I admitted to myself that I was causing the problem, I walked upstairs and Mother said, "Daughter, you can go out into the world anytime you want to and do your work."

You all so want to blame the other guy. "He did it. She did it. He's doing it to me. She's doing it to me." You could all have said no, couldn't you? We can always say no. There is such a word.

Somebody wanted me to tell the old story about the library card. It fits tonight's theme of tenacity of purpose. I was walking with a shiny purse in a bad part of Oakland, where I was living in a studio that was a converted stable in the garden of a mansion. In Santa Barbara, somebody had told me that when the Earth begins to go back on its axis, it is our duty to send love into Mother Earth. I was so struck by it that I always had it in my mind that if the Earth went back on its axis, I would send love into Mother Earth.

So all at once, walking home, I started to sway from side to side, and I thought, this is Mother Earth going back on her axis, so I must send love into her. I swung back and forth and back and forth until I looked down and I found all I had of my purse was the handle. Somebody had been sawing it off, and as he sawed, I was swaying. I was so horror-struck. I yelled after the man, who was running, "Don't run. You can have it. You can have it. Don't run. You can have my purse!"

Then I got to thinking about the Masters. I had been thinking of the Masters and walking along with my head in the sky and my feet in the sky, too. I belly-ached at the Masters saying, "Why didn't you tell me someone was behind me?" I didn't even know there was anyone there sawing my purse until I saw him running a block away. You can see where I was. I wasn't very grounded, do you understand? So I said, "I think it was a dirty trick, that's all I can say." They got very stern then, and they said, "You had no right to walk with a big purse, a shiny patent-leather purse, in that part of town. You therefore have made karma for the man who stole your purse."

I listened to that. I went up into my studio, and I started thinking about what was in my purse. I didn't care about the money because I didn't have any. I didn't have any credit cards because I've never had one in my life, even to this day. All at once I remembered my library card. Like you with your credit cards, see? I said, "He took my library card! He took my library card! God, you let him take my library card! God, you let him take my library card!" For three days I went on, "God, you let him take my library card!" I visualized him taking absolutely dozens of books out on my library card.

You could only take out five. For ten cents, I could have made a phone call and said, "My library card has been stolen," but I didn't dwell in that space, you understand, and still don't. I'm still nutty.

I went on for three days with tenacity of purpose until that tenacity of purpose did something. I was walking in a place where there were no buildings, no trees, no nothing, just blue sky, and I saw a little piece of paper coming down, coming down in a circular way, and it fell at my feet. In curiosity I picked it up, and it was my library card. Tenacity of purpose, do you understand? You have to have that if you want something to come to pass.

I could go on with more stories like that. This is another nice story. I never talked about my beliefs or proselytized about them. One day I was in the studio and a woman came running in hysterically and said, "My daughter" — a dancer who danced with me — "is across the street dying in the hospital." At that moment I was lying in bed feeling very ill. I looked at her and said, "I'll get dressed and come. You go back to your daughter."

As I came out of my room, Jan Mauser, who was one of those who lived in the studio, came out of his room. I said, "Jan, how can I go? Look at the mess I'm in. I feel sick. I'm a mess, and she wants me to go and save her daughter. That's absolutely nuts. What can I do?" Jan wasn't into our thing at all. I remember him smoking a cigarette and drinking a glass of wine most of the time, drawing pictures, playing the piano and having a nice time on this Earth while I was striving and striving. But he said, "Hilda, Saint Paul had an affliction, and he healed. Get dressed and go over there." I listened to him and I went. I told the girl's mother to hold one hand and I held the other, and the result was that she started to breathe and she's alive to this day. I used to get Christmas cards from her.

You see, there was unworthiness in me. Do you follow me? Don't let unworthiness spoil your work. Don't let yourself feel that you are unworthy. Saint Paul didn't think he was unworthy, so think of Saint Paul when a feeling of unworthiness comes on you. The Bible says he had some affliction so he could have gone and never done anything because of that affliction. So don't let unworthiness get you. I had unworthiness, but I went over there anyway. I overcame it.

As for your advancement, kids, I would say you were very well along the path, most of you who have been coming to me. But if God told you how advanced you were, what would happen to you? Ego. You'd be saying, "I'm spiritual — I am spirit-u-elle." I didn't know I'd gotten anywhere at all, not at all, until I got to India. Then I would go to the spiritual masters, and I found that they gave me extra attention. Now whether it was because I was extra dumb or because I had made something of myself, I don't know, but I took it as the second one. That was the only time I knew that I had really gained anything with all these years of suffering that I had over here in this country. So if you feel that you've gotten nowhere, then know you're getting somewhere. Know that you have something in there and keep enough ego to say, "I can make it. If that singer made it, I can make it. If that painter made it, I can make it." Whatever books you've read about people who made it, remember them and say, "I can do it because God created me in His image and likeness."

I'm going to speak a little on Joan of Arc. As I've told you many times, I was a very timid child. At four years of age, whirling wheels would come inside me, and I'd go screaming to my mother. They were the chakras opening up. I would go to my mother and say, "Those colors, those wheels, those colors." She'd say, "Oh, what colors?" I didn't get much sympathy. Everything scared me so I was very, very timid about people, just a kind of a nincompoop, I guess.

Mother was always doing theatricals when we were in Salt Lake City. We were not Mormons, but they asked my dad and mother to do theatricals. One time she did a pageant about all the nations, and I represented France in a crummy Joan of Arc outfit. I'd never heard of Joan of Arc. I didn't even know what I was representing. Then, as I stood on the stage, I heard from way up in the sky, "Je suis Jeanne d'Arc — I am Joan of Arc. My strength I give unto thee, to fight your battle on Earth with faith and forbearance as I fought mine. I am with thee to the end." Then I saw a great ribbon of light come down, flash down like a power, and enter me.

I didn't think much about it because I never made a great deal of thinking about anything of this Earth or of any of its happenings, but I found out that something had happened to me. Until then, when mother would ask me to go down the street to pick up something at the little store, the boy there would stick out his tongue, and I would run like mad as if he had a dagger or something. After that I went and just stood and looked at him, and he ran as if I were going to shoot him with a machine gun. Every time I went past his house from then on, he just ran. Something had happened to me with that power that had gone into me. From that moment, I had a lot of strength and belief and power.

Joan of Arc was born in 1412. Because I can remember some of my lives, I know that at that time I was on Earth as a nun named Colette. If in a future life I think back into this present incarnation, one of the most wonderful moments was standing in the middle of Stonehenge. The guards let me go in and stand inside the circle, and it was magical. It was out of this world. It was so wonderful. I think also of being with my guru, Nityananda, and his bliss that he gave me. And being with Sathya Sai Baba. But in all my incarnations the most wonderful moment of all was when I stood as Colette in the 1400s and saw the Maid go by — Jeanne d'Arc. Everybody yelled, "The Maid, the Maid, the Maid's coming — the Maid, the Maid, the Maid, the Maid." The air rang with it. That was my greatest moment. Perhaps that's why she came to me in this life. Otherwise I don't know why she would choose a stupid little girl like me. It was so wonderful — "The Maid, the Maid, the Maid!"

She is very dear to me. I don't know how to tell you how dear she is to me and has been through this whole life. From the time her power entered me, I knew everything she suffered. I knew what it was like to be shackled. I knew what it was like to be tied to a bed with men in the room. For a long time, if we went to a theater, I had to sit on the end seat; otherwise, I felt I was incarcerated. This thing entered me so terrifically. Whatever happened, along with the grace she gave, she also gave the suffering. In that life I did meet her, I am so proud to say. In that life, she visited the convent in which I lived. It says so in the books. I suppose she always asked the convents to pray for her, and I suppose in that life, I prayed. I suppose that when she came to me in this life, she was paying back her debt. I don't know.

What would you tell us of life, my Joan? What would you say this night from your place up there where all is light? What would you say to us who fight the fight down here in this world of chaos and darkness and despair? What would you say to us, Joan? You fought as a soldier on Earth, but the fight was for Truth — a warrior of God who stood undaunted with feet on the Earth, head in the sky. What matter they burned your body and for one fleeting second in eternity pain filled your being?

Do you know that when they went to take her ashes away, they found her heart intact? They couldn't burn her heart. It was as fresh as if it were beating inside her. They took it and threw it in the river so there would be nothing left that anyone could venerate.

What matter they burned your body? For one fleeting second in eternity, pain filled your being. The truth, the courage, the power, the love you left as a heritage on the Earth remain forever for those who will to be free from the tyrants within.

The tyrants within us — the gossip, the ugliness, the meanness, the hates — give them up, kids. Give them up before God forces you to.

You freed France, Joan, and we want to free ourselves. You fought with indomitable will, the will of God, to show us the ills of the Earth, the ills that beset man and woman on Earth. Strong and gentle were your ways, never faltering — only perhaps faltering for one second in eternity. They wanted her to say something for which she would have escaped the stake. She didn't want to be burned. She was young, nineteen. Who wants to be burned in fire? For one moment she faltered and lied, but then she came back again and said, "Yes, I saw the angels, and all I said is true," gaining back more strength because of that faltering space. They often say that Jesus knelt on the ground and said to his Father, "Will You take this cup from me?" I don't think he did. That sounds silly to me, but they do say that.

You lived in faith, Joan, innocent enough to believe what you heard. Untainted you were. Born untainted, you returned to your high domain in the heavenly world from which you had descended to show Truth to us all. Show us undaunted faith so we can look into your life as a true mirror of ourselves — our golden God who dwells within.

If some voice came to us — oh, let's say a voice came to me and said I was to go to Reagan and tell him I was going to take over the Army and the Navy — I don't think I'd go. First of all, I wouldn't get through the gates of the White House. But when the voice told Joan to go, she went. At Lourdes, when the Mother said to Bernadette, "Drink of the spring," she looked around and she couldn't find one. All she saw was some wet mud. She poked the mud in her mouth to obey. Would we do that? Have we that much faith? Have we that much courage? If we don't, then let's get it!

You are unique, Joan. You can be measured by the standards of time without misgiving or apprehension. I hesitate not to glorify you in your life. It was flawless. It is still ideally perfect. It occupies a lofty place of attainment. "A loftier one could not be reached by any other mere mortal," says Mark Twain.[3] Mere mortal. He's not talking of prophets and avatars. He continues, "She was truthful when lying was the common speech of [humankind]..." Think of how it is now upon this Earth. The same conditions exist.

> She was honest when honesty had become a lost virtue;
> she was a keeper of promises when the keeping of promises
> was expected of no one; she gave her mind to great
> thoughts and great purposes when other great minds
> wasted themselves upon petty fancies or upon poor ambi-
> tions...

Don't let your minds be small, kids, with pettiness and gossip.

> She was modest and fine, and delicate when to be loud
> and coarse might be said to be universal; she was full of
> pity when a merciless cruelty was the rule; she was stead-
> fast when stability was unknown, and honorable in an age
> which had forgotten what honor was; she was a rock of
> conviction in a time when men believed in nothing and
> scoffed at all things.

Very much like now, isn't it? We've got to be Joan of Arcs.

> She was unfailingly true in an age that was false to the
> core; she maintained her personal dignity unimpaired in
> an age of fawnings and servilities; she was of a dauntless
> courage when hope and courage had perished in the hearts
> of her nation. She was spotlessly pure in mind and body
> when society in the highest places was foul in both — she
> was all these things in an age when crime was common
> business of the lords and princes, and when the highest
> personages in Christendom were able to astonish even that
> infamous era and make it stand aghast at the spectacle of
> their atrocious lives.

It could be now that he was talking about.

> She was perhaps the only entirely unselfish person
> whose name has a place in profane history. She was offered
> rewards and honors, but she refused them all, and would
> take nothing. All she would take for herself — if the King
> would grant it — was leave to go back to her village home
> and tend her sheep again.

When he said, "What do you want, Joan?" she said, "I just want to go home
and tend my sheep." Of course, she couldn't.

> The selfishness of the Maid, an ideal of an applauding

nation, reached only that far, the desire to return home to
her village and be forgotten, no further.

Joan of Arc, a mere child in years, ignorant, unlettered,...
without influence, found a great nation...in chains, help-
less and hopeless,...its treasury bankrupt, its soldiers dis-
heartened... all spirit torpid, all courage dead...and she laid
her hand upon this nation, this corpse, and it rose and
followed her.

Those rough soldiers followed her, and she said they had to pray every
morning. All they knew was womanizing and cursing. One person living
true to God can change a world. One man, one woman, living true to God
can change the destiny of a world.

She fatally crippled the English power, and died with
the earned title of Deliverer of France, which she bears to
this day. And for all reward, the French King, whom she
had crowned, stood supine and indifferent, while French
priests took the noble child, the most innocent, the most
lovely, the most adorable the ages had produced, and
burned her alive at the stake.[4]

That age is our own time. Those in the heavens beseech us in the midst
of this dark age to live as a gleam of light.

I asked Joan of Arc if she could talk to us now, what would she say? She
said:

I lived true unto my destiny with courage, but courage
without faith is like storming the fortress at the wrong
time.

Did you get that? If you have courage and push through, it isn't enough
unless you've got faith. With faith comes wisdom.

To do without faith or act without faith in God is to
flounder in the dark. I walked upon the Earth a short time,
played my part and left the scene, but the fragrance of my
life of faith in God remains for those who have the simplicity to take of this inspiration.

I hope many of you will take of this inspiration this night because she
will be with you through all that is to come.

I left God's heritage of truth and courage, faith, fortitude
and love upon this Earth. That is the most that a man or

woman can expect to do.

That is the most we can leave here, kids. We know when we come in that we're going to pass on. Leave something here, but don't leave gossip, don't leave pettiness. Please, I beg of you.

> Life is fleeting and soon fades away, but the truth of living lives on forever, a path for others to walk upon. Such was my short stay upon this Earth. I moved upon the Earth, paused a while, and returned from whence I came. I never died.

Let us contemplate the words of Joan and sit quietly, backs straight. Let's breathe into our heart centers. Do it yourself, breathing in and out of your heart center. This night let courage be given to you as a gift — courage to go forward in life, courage that you are an individual who can change your bit in the world.

Believe in yourself. Do the impossible. Lighten the way with a smile, a cheerful word. It matters not whether worldly fame has come your way, but let not shame or unworthiness dampen your spirits. Live undaunted, my kids, true unto yourself. Peace will fill your inner self then. Be true to Self and you are true to God, to life, to all. Take courage into yourself this moment. Take of this gift this night. Take of fortitude, but, above all, take faith.

When in exile wandering, lost and knowing not which way we should turn, we shall almost fainting yearn and yearn for just a glimpse, a sign from thee, O Maid of Light and Truth. Oh, then, Joan, don't let us down.

Rise upon our sight, O Joan, this moment.

Please bring your focus to your forehead. Let us go back in time just for a moment, back to France, and stand upon French soil and once again hear in the distance, "The Maid, the Maid, she comes!" See her on a big white horse riding past. That is all that is needed. Let the perfume of her soul fill all around. We know we have seen a glimpse of heaven's light.

This night, O Joan, send down your rays to help us all and to bring forth from our inner selves the power to go through all that is to come. We will remember you, O Joan, and dauntless be, for you have paved the roads and cleared the paths so we can see the horizon and know that just ahead our dreams of peace, of love, of truth are there.

Hold high your banner and march before us, Joan. Let us glimpse that waving banner in the wind and know that if we believe in God and in ourselves, we are bound to win; we cannot lose. When times are hard and the clouds seem to dim the sky and we don't know which way to turn, where to live, where to get money or food, let us each have faith and courage and believe that God knows what He is doing. Give us all a banner that we can glimpse within our hands and use to clear the sky. Let all the obstacles of all those here and the darkness in their lives fade before this banner which we hold. I shall hold it high, right this moment. We shall win, for we have Joan as our model and Saint Therese the Little Flower. Did not Anne Frank say, "I still believe that people are really good at heart"? Anne Frank, whom I classify with Joan of Arc, as I do Saint Therese, said, "I simply cannot build up my hopes on a foundation consisting of confusion, misery and death. I see the world gradually being turned into a wilderness. I hear the ever-approaching thunder which will destroy us." No, it will not, I say! Anne Frank, I change it. I say, no, it will not destroy us! She says, "I can feel the sufferings of millions and yet if I look up into the heavens, I think it will all come right, that this cruelty will end and that peace and tranquility will return again. In the meantime, I must hold my ideals and perhaps the time will come when I will be able to carry them out."[5] Anne Frank, I'm sure you will. Joan of Arc, you've carried yours out. Little Flower, you wrote your book.

Let's just sit quietly for a moment. "The Maid. The Maid." Everything that goes into the ethers stays there. I went down to France to see Colette's place, and we stayed at a nearby hotel in Amiens. As I lay in bed, I heard "Marchons, marchons!" and I saw crowds waving and waving and waving flags. I saw a man, an old soldier who didn't know he was dead, come into my room, and I said, "What do you want? Please go." I heard this "Marchons, marchons!" like I heard "The Maid, the Maid!" These glorious things stay forever. I went downstairs in the hotel and I asked, "Was this part of the land in the war?" They said, "Yes, Patton came through here to save France." They sang "Marchons, marchons!" for Patton. It was still in the ethers and I could hear it being sung. Everything we put in the ethers remains there. Let's not cover our fellow man or fellow woman with darkness, gossip, pettiness.

Oh, I plead with you, live to your highest. Live to the greatness in yourself, to the God within you. Live to the glory of the God that dwells within you. If you have your feet on the ground, keep your head in the sky. I ask of you, do not lose the vision of heaven. Please. We must stay in the heaven world in our mind. We must know that a great world is coming. We cannot live in the horror of the lower world.

Be stalwart and live to your highest. Be strong, have faith, and come through. This is the lowest ebb of the world. It cannot go any lower, thank God. It's on its upward trend now, and we shall fly up with it.

Don't have any doubts in yourself any more. Believe in yourself and in God and make it through.

Chapter Five

Divine Hints
For Spiritual Growth

You should never lose faith in your innate perfection. Believe in yourself, but first have complete faith in God, who knows what He is doing. Innate means inborn, and the Lord can bring it forth.

Innate perfection means that perfection within you that has never been touched since the time it was created. It is perfect inside of you — no matter what wrongs you've done, what sins you've committed. It is a spot inside you that is as white as snow.

That perfection is what you have to bring forth and expand into the rest of you. That is what Jesus was talking about all the time — bringing the perfection forth. That is why he went on the cross and why the prophets of all religions, out of compassion, came down to us. They all spoke the same message: perfection is within us. They came down to Earth to teach us this truth.

Find this spot inside you now. Close your eyes for one moment and grab hold of it. Say, "I've got this innate perfection inside me. Nobody has ever touched it. No divorces, no troubles, no lovers, no diseases, nothing has touched it."

At this moment, something comes to my mind — a child that you may have read about. At the age of three he went into a coma. For years he was fed artificially. At eight, just when they were going to pull out the plug, he opened his eyes and he said to his mother, "I have been in paradise." He described heaven. He said, "I met grandma and grandpa." He described them. He had never met them on Earth because they had passed on before he could meet them. He had been up there all those years. He said, "I just came down to say goodbye and to tell you that I'm in paradise, and I will meet you when you come up." And he passed on.

It is a beautiful story, is it not? It is a story of courage and strength for someone to come down and tell how beautiful it is up there so that when a loved one passes on, you don't grieve, but you feel happy. In the Orient, when an older person passes on, they have a funeral with horns blowing and a band playing, because they say they're going on to a glory. But here we don't let go.

That story has nothing to do with our lesson except that I thought it was lovely and very inspiring.

The Earth at this time is so darkened with meanness and hate. Sometimes I can't stand to stay down here on Earth with all the gossip and all the smallness of people and the meanness of them. Then I remember your smiling faces and your trust, and I look at the spiritual growth that has happened to all of you who have been coming for a long time. I know your spiritual growth has happened in the midst of the darkness, and I yell "No!" to the heavens and say, "I'm staying down here!" And I gather my perseverance and my tenacity and I mix it with love and strength and cover myself with this protective force. And I'm off to a new start.

Cheap gossip is what causes so much trouble. The creative energy comes up the spine and is supposed to go on up, but it comes out of the mouth as toads instead of diamonds — toads of gossip. The Masters hate it. I'd like to show you a new and correct way to gossip. Watch this.

Brian: Robert, how are you doing?

Robert: Great, Brian. How are you doing?

Brian: Fine, thanks. Hey, I've got some really heavy duty juicy gossip.

Robert: Hey, heavy duty juicy gossip!

Brian: This is major stuff. This could keep people out of the New Age if it weren't New Age gossip.

Robert: Just a minute, Brian. Hold on. (*Aside to audience:* Immediately after the meeting I'm going to tell you everything!) What were you saying, Brian?

Brian: Okay, this is New Age gossip. The thing about it is, I'm going to tell you all the dirty stuff about myself.

Robert: About yourself?

Brian: About myself. Ready?

Robert: All right.

Brian: Okay. First of all, people think that I don't react when Hilda corrects me. Right?

Robert: Right.

Brian: Well, I react constantly to Hilda. Hilda comes up to me and goes, "Brian, are you angry at so-and-so?" And I go, "No, Hilda, I'm not angry." Meanwhile, my face is turning red, and my legs are shaking, but I don't want her to know that I'm really angry. If I had anger in me, then she might not let me help her with the microphone. It could be bad business. But I do sometimes get angry.

Robert: Okay, now, that's fine, but give me the real juicy gossip. Come on. I want to hear it all. (*Aside to the audience:* I'll tell you later.)

Brian: But it's about me. This is New Age gossip. Here's the other scoop. Now, people think I'm a decent meditator even though I got married this year. But forget it! I haven't had concentration in the last six years. Hilda says you're supposed to take in the light from God, right, God's nutrients? Well, in a typical meditation I take in a lot of nutrients — about eight dinners. I go to all these different restaurants. Forget it. I mean, I'm really not a good meditator.

Robert: This is the juicy gossip you wanted to tell me about yourself?

Brian: Yeah, this is the juicy gossip. I'm full of all kinds of junk and rot. You remember the movie "Star Wars," when they're in this garbage chute, and all these little snakes and stuff are swimming around?

Robert: I remember.

Brian: And this bug-eyed monster comes out and tries to grab Luke? Those guys are in me.

Robert: You're kidding!

Brian: I'm serious.

Robert: And you're telling me about it. New Age gossip. What an incredible concept. (*Aside to audience:* I'm not

going to tell any of you a thing. I'm keeping this one to
myself. My lips are sealed.)

That's New Age gossip. If you have to tell any gossip, tell it about
yourself. You understand? And tell it to somebody who is not going to
spread the news about you either. Don't gossip any more, kids. It's so sad
for me. It comes back to my ears. I feel it in my bones when you're doing it.
It's horrible. The Masters said that cheap gossip is what makes trouble.

I was put through a test once. This yogi said, "You are not to talk until I
give you permission," and then he started a lecture of two hours. All I
wanted to do was to interrupt him. I just went on holding my mouth shut,
and I got through those two hours. He came up and said, "Well done!"

It's very hard to stop the misuse of Creative Power because the Creative
Power is so strong. It's so powerful it could blow up a city. When it comes
out of the mouth, it should come out in goodness and kindness and prayers.

In a way the world is divided into two parts. The upper, or higher, part
of the world is all about God, saints, Hierarchy, meditation and prayers. The
lower part is also God, but it is the testing ground to see if you can stay in
the higher thoughts and feelings or if you fall down. Do you understand
this? If we didn't have this test, we wouldn't know whether we could
remain detached from the world and stay up there. I tell you, it's darn hard
to stay up in the higher world when that lower mind is going on inside you
on all those subjects: "I lost my job. This happened. That happened." You
try to say, "No, no, no — I'm going to think about Mary, I'm going to think
about God, about Moses parting the sea." But your mind keeps going, "And
that job..." and you wake up in the middle of the night thinking, "That job..."

The two things are going on at the same time. So to stay up there, you
have to get a mantra. Every time your mind is going around and around
down here, you're doing harm to yourself and the world. So what you can
do is this: you say something about up there. Think of a color. If you can't
do anything else, think "purple, purple, purple." Purple is the highest color
there is. It's Count Saint Germaine's.

Did you notice I have a ring on? I haven't worn a ring for twenty, thirty,
forty years, except the one Sai Baba made for me. But somebody wanted to
give me this, and it reminds me of Count Saint Germaine. I said, "I'll take it
if I can pay for the material and you make it." So we made a deal. Every time
I look at it, I say, "Count Saint Germaine, Count Saint Germaine, purple,
purple, gold, gold of Lazumma." Say some things like that to take you out

of that other world.

When I listen to TV evangelists, it is like this to me: when they say all those wonderful things about Jesus, they are speaking from up above. But if they are speaking from down below, like they do every once in awhile — they may say Isis is Satan, Buddhists are nothing — then I ignore that part. I've turned the TV on to hear about the higher part, so why should I react to the lower part? If I want to hear about a Buddhist, I'll turn to another program and find somebody with an orange robe on. If I want a Jewish program, which I often listen to, I'll turn to another station. If I want to hear about Jesus, I'll turn to an evangelist. If the evangelist says all these mean things down here, that's his problem, not my problem. You've got it? Just stop criticizing everything. Keep your feet on the earth and your head in the sky.

Here are three rules for keeping yourself out of the dregs of the Earth. By so doing, you will open the gate to the Golden Age and dance into the Golden Age, not crawl on your belly in the dust, asking Christ's forgiveness for your sins. You'll dance in.

Number one is watch your tongue. It is an instrument God created to enable you to communicate through sound with your brothers and sisters on Earth with love, not with gossip and hatred and quarreling. Every word you utter creates. Be aware as you speak and think, and ask yourself, "Do I want this created in my life?" Let only the highest words, thoughts and truth come from your tongue from this day onward. Speak words that are true, kind and helpful. Often things are true, but they are not very kind and they're not very helpful. Now is your time to start, from this day onward.

You have to understand that far up in the unmanifest world, there is an ocean of God of sound, an ocean out of which sounds will come, sounds that are not words. Imagine a line where on one side is the manifest world and on the other the unmanifest world. In the beginning the sound is let through to the manifest world a little at a time. I'll make some of the sounds. It will have meaning to those of the upper world, but no meaning to you except as you feel it. I'll do a Mayan chant that I learned from the ethers. I met a lady, an anthropologist, who had been to the interior of Central America, and I asked her, "What are these chants that I'm saying?" She said, "It's ancient Mayan — ancient, ancient Mayan." I will chant it for you. [Hilda chants]

The sound comes down from the unmanifest. It comes down to the realm of Gods, where they speak in poetry. Then it comes down lower to the Masters, where they speak almost archaic English. Then it gets down to us where we're saying four-letter words to each other. When I go into the ladies' lavatories, I see some beauties on the walls and doors. When it gets down here, we take that glorious sound and bring it lower and lower and lower until all we're saying are ugly words at each other: "Shut up! Come on! You don't mean that!" Everything comes down into something ugly instead of into beautiful sounds. If I got on the bus and did that Mayan chant, they would say, "Put your money in the box." We have to talk, but let's talk good sounds and cut out the gossip.

When somebody tells me, "I heard this about so-and-so, but I won't tell you who said it," what does that mean? They are upholding the gossiper against me and against all of you. They are protecting the gossiper instead of saying to the gossiper, "Please don't tell me that. I'd have to tell who said it in order to be honest, so please don't talk about it." Let's get some of those higher sounds in our lives, shall we?

Here's the second rule. Think the highest thoughts, and let the fearful, the lowest and the degrading thoughts of yourself and others be harnessed until a habit of godly positivity and spirituality prevails. Think good of yourself. Say, "I've got an innate perfection in myself. Hilda says so and that's all there is to it. Shut up, you dummy inside me." If it starts saying, "Oh no, you haven't," say, "Shut up." Or you might chant. That might take you up higher.

Again, think the highest thoughts and let the fearful, the low and the degrading thoughts of yourself and others be harnessed. Harness them! Harness them like a horse that has to walk on a road, until there remain only thoughts of godly truth. This is a necessity to enable the body to take on immortality. It's a necessity so these atoms can get finer. As they get finer, it's going to be harder living in this world for a while. Then you'll be writing letters to me saying, "I'm a mess. I'm so sensitive. I don't know what to do. My kundalini is rising." I'll just say, "Let it rise."

Forget the evil past, remember the good, and you will find ananda, or bliss, flowing through you. Every time you start thinking of some awful thing you did — it will come out of the subconscious — you say, "Bliss supreme, ananda is mine."

Sathya Sai Baba promised me that if I remained in India with him, he would give me ananda the rest of my life. But I chose to come over here and be with you people. Was I a fool? No! What would I have done over there? I couldn't sit on my behind just doing nothing.

Think on nothing or no one. Let each moment be the beginning of the new. The beginning of the new — easy to say, harder to do. But with perseverance you will find that it gets easier and smoother. Make it a habit until it becomes your life. Then you need not worry that the UFOs will leave you behind, because you will be an asset to the new world about to come forth, and they will pick you up for sure. In fact, the UFOs, or Brothers of Light, will have you coded in and will know just where you are so they can save you. What does "coded in" mean? Does that scare you? Are they going to give us a number on our wrist or something? No! On their screen, which I often see, they know just where you are. The Masters know where you are at all times. If an earthquake were coming, they would know just where you are, just where your children are, where your husband is, where everybody is, so you will be protected.

You must stop the nonsense. Don't think the Brothers of Light want gossipers or gossip-listeners or hateful, malicious people up in their world. Nothing doing! They are not going to take any of those up there. They will code you out. They have four billion people to choose from. Out of that many, they can find a few good ones. I hope it is you. I know it is you. Remember when the UFO appeared above the Cathedral spires after class and sightings were reported that night on network news? They didn't come over our church to look us over for nothing, did they? They almost hit the spire. They came to look us over to see if there were any good ones down here. They said, "Yeah, there are a lot of good ones down there."

Now here is number three. Act unselfishly and lovingly at all times in even the smallest events. Watch your thoughts, and don't let greed into your mind or heart. Remember that if hate from others comes your way, send back love that breaks up the dark clouds. Send back love, love, love, until those hate clouds, those black magic clouds, just break up and disperse. Send back love, love, love. It's hard, but go on doing it. You breathe in and you breathe out from your center, and you disperse the cloud of malicious hatred that comes your way sometimes. For you are a Master. You are a Daughter of Light.

When these three rules are established in your lives, you will rise above the darkness, the tribulation and futility on Earth at this time, and you will live to experience the glory of Christ that your hearts have longed for. From the very beginning of time, you've longed for this perfection, which is yours if you do these things with your tongue, your thoughts and your actions.

The next thing I would like to take up with you is the quieting of the mind, because that is the difficulty that most people have in meditation. When you meditate, all sorts of things come into your mind. So I am going to show you how to still yourself.

Take your right thumb and put it on your right nostril. Inhale through your left nostril. Hold by putting your right middle finger and ring finger against your left nostril. And releasing the right thumb, breathe out the right nostril. Repeat, using the same technique. Breathe in your right nostril. Hold, and breathe out your left, smoothly. Let it flow out on the word love. Now breathe in the left nostril, and see a golden love energy flowing into your mind. Hold it there. Let it saturate every atom of your mind. Breathe it out through the right nostril and let it flow over the world.

Now breathe into the heart center, as if you have a set of nostrils right in the center of your chest. Fill up your mind and body with love, saturating every atom. Now breathe love out into the world. Let it flow out like a wave of beautiful golden light. Now draw it in again through the nostrils on the chest, smoothly, filling every atom of the mind, seeing that golden love power saturating every atom. Send it out softly, smoothly, masterfully. Now again draw it in. Take your time. Be aware. Hold the breath for a second. Now send it out to someone else.

Do this every day of your life. This will balance your body, and when you go into deep meditation, you will be able to come out of it very easily. Try it this moment and see which nostril you're breathing the most out of. Every hour it changes. A good yogi will do this breathing out of both all of the time.

This is a preparation for the day that you can do in the morning for about five minutes. It will get your mind under control and your breath under control.

Now, the next part. I'm going to give you ideas that you can think on. Close your eyes. You're going to talk to yourself. This is the way you're going to do it. It's going to be just as if I were talking to you and you were repeating to yourself, inside yourself:

> I am sitting in a forest. I can hear a waterfall in the
> distance. I can hear the ripple of a river.

Talk to yourself. Say:

Now I'm going to float down that river. I'm going to get
on a little rubber dingy. I'm going to sit on it, and I'm going
to float down this river.

Hear the ripples of the water.

I'm going to dip my hand into the water and feel the
coolness of it.

Come on, do it if you're interested in meditation.

Now look to the left and see the trees slowly going by. Look to the right
and see the daffodils blowing in the wind. In the distance, you hear the roar
of the ocean of God because you're wending your way toward it.

That's the way you talk to yourself in meditation in the beginning to keep
your mind from straying.

Now this moment feel as if you cannot feel your feet on the floor, nor
your body sitting on the floor or in the chair, because you have gone into a
higher state. It is almost as if your body has disappeared and you've gone
into another body, a higher body, your causal body. So you talk like this to
yourself — say it to yourself now out loud:

I am coming down. I am coming down. I am breathing
normally. I am coming down. The Divine Mother, kundalini inside me, knows how to take me to God. I wiggle
my toes. I move my fingers. I will open my eyes, a new me.
No harm can come to me.

All right, open your eyes. Now that is a sample of what you do when you
begin to meditate and concentrate, instead of sitting there for ten minutes
and saying, "I wonder if I'm going to miss the bus? I wonder what I'm going
to have for breakfast. I can smell breakfast. It's burning!" In a meditation,
teach yourself how to think. Do you understand that clearly? Just talk to
yourself. You don't have to talk about forests; you can talk about something
else. You can talk about heavenly kingdoms. You can talk about Skanda. You
can talk about anything you want, but keep your mind busy until such time
as you get quiet. When you can't feel your body don't say, "Oh my God,
I've lost my body. I've lost my body." What you say is, "If I can think that
I've lost my body, then I haven't lost it, have I?" So you say, "I'm coming
down. I'm breathing nicely, in and out, in and out. I'm coming down. I'm
coming down." And then pretty soon you say, "Oh, I wiggle my toes. The
blood is flowing through my veins, making me alive and vital."

Stay away from seeking psychic phenomena, but if a vision comes, challenge it in the name of Jesus. I use that name because he was a great Master at getting rid of the negative. You just say, "In the name of Jesus, who are you?" You say it three times. Even if it is Jesus or Moses that you are seeing in your vision, they won't get mad. They'll say, "Smart person."

You may have darshan of many saints. They come in a flash — boom! And you say, "Did I see somebody or didn't I see somebody? Was that Saint Therese? Was that Sai Baba? Who was it that went by so fast?" It's very fast, the darshan, but it means they've blessed you — even if it's just a flick. And you say, "Who could it be? I've got to get a book and look it up." You look it up, and you find out who it was that came and blessed you. They don't hang around when they come to bless you. It's real fast.

Let's do a few affirmations, affirmations that can keep you positive. We're all going to repeat: "I will build a wall of light around myself that nothing can penetrate. I will build a wall of light around myself that nothing can penetrate. I will build a wall of light around myself that nothing can penetrate. I am indestructible, perfect. I am indestructible, perfect. I am indestructible, perfect."

Once when I was going out of my body, zooming out to another planet, I heard a very loud sound. They were testing me. I said, "I am indestructible, perfect." I opened my eyes and came back into my body, and I said, "I am indestructible, perfect. I am indestructible, perfect. I am indestructible, perfect." Keep that in your mind. We are indestructible, perfect.

Find the age in your life you love the best, when it was the most fun. Come on, close your eyes. The age you love the best. I am fifteen years of age, or I am ten, or five, or three. Think of that age. So when you get up in the morning, you say, for example, "I am twenty-four years of age, and I am going to be twenty-four for the rest of my life." That keeps the aliveness in you. Find the age you like, before all your troubles started, before you got your worries, before you started to know about reincarnation and everything. Go back to an age when you were free. When you get up in the morning, you can say, "I am four years of age. I am full of fun, no worries, no fears, no cares, no nothing. I am four years of age." Every morning when you get up, say that same age — don't change it. The power of it will build up in you. All the fun you had before your troubles started will build up again in you.

Let's see. Let's have some more affirmations: "We will conquer, we will conquer, we will conquer with love. We will persevere, we will persevere, we will persevere with strength. I am free, I am free, I am free."

Now I'll show you what to do to really get the negative out of your innards. When you're feeling like you've been bumped and bothered and you've got all this junk in your body, you say four times: "I am free, I am free, I am free!" Say "I am free!" twelve times in all.

Just relax in God now. Relax your shoulders. Relax every part of you. Relax into your inner Self.

At the end of each season of classes, I try to speak of those who have meant much to me in this life and other lives. Many who are psychic must have seen Pericles here, along with the other Masters, standing above us and on the stage. Pericles always wears his Grecian outfit. He never takes it off. Although Pericles was a general, he sponsored democracy and the arts. Athens attained her greatest height during the thirty years or more that he was the head statesman. Pericles sincerely contemplated the good of his fellow countrymen, and he endeavored to realize an ideal Athens where people were free and had an intelligent obedience to an equitable code of law.

You don't know it, but you have been drawn here from ancient Greece. You have within you the seed that was called the Periclean Golden Age, and now we're going into a new Golden Age. You may not remember you lived there, but I've slowly drawn here those of you who belonged to that in the past and still have that dream inside of you.

Pericles had great influence on the arts of the time. He rebuilt the Parthenon and put the great sculptor Phidias in charge of designing the great sixty-foot statue of Athena that was covered with gold leaf inside the Parthenon. He accomplished all that he started out to do with his calm and undaunted attitude of mind, which he preserved in the midst of the severest trials. Just as Skanda is compared with Shiva, Pericles was commonly compared to the Olympian God Zeus because of his serene and dignified bearing and his eloquence, with which he held both friend and foe spellbound.

Right now, see this great man standing straight, wearing his helmet. One cannot speak of Pericles without speaking of the great ones who were his friends, such as Herodotus the historian, the great philosophers Anaxagoras and Socrates, and Aspasia. We owe whatever democracy we have at this time to Pericles: he started it during the Golden Age. We also owe him our great theaters, our poetry, our plays, our music, our art.

There was a seed that was sown at that time into our hearts. That's why we long for this new age to come, for this Age of Gold to come. That's why we can't stand things as they are now, because that seed was sown in us.

We cannot speak of Pericles without speaking of Aspasia, who was a great influence at that time. She was like the first women's-libber. The women of that time were like chattel. They were kept in another part of the house, where they bore the children, took care of the servants, saw that the cooking was done right, while the men had all the fun in the front room. Aspasia said, "We'll put a stop to that!" She started a school where she taught wealthy young girls until they were about sixteen. They were allowed to mix with men because they were intelligent. She taught them everything — poetry, art, history, mathematics.

Aspasia was not originally from Athens, but came from Miletus, which was in Persia. Those who were interested in art and the furtherance of humanity had gathered together in Athens. They had heard about Athens and said, "We've got to go there. That's where the art is. That's where we can expand ourselves. That's where we can do our thing." When Aspasia was about fifteen or sixteen years of age, she got on a sailing boat, her blue cape flying in the wind, and went to Athens to fulfill her destiny in the Golden Age. She was beautiful of body as well as of mind and played an important part in the life of Pericles and in the lives of the artists and sculptors of the time. She was one of the few women who mixed with these men of great minds. She sat with them as they all planned the Parthenon; she sat with them as they all planned the theaters, as they created their arts.

I wish to give Pericles full honor this night, as I do each year because he belongs to the Masters. Although he is not one of their group, he mixes with them. He is perfect, a Perfected Being. If you should have troubles fighting your lower nature, if you're fighting your sexual energies and you want to raise them up, or if you want your mind to become cleaner, call Pericles' name. He is perfect even as Skanda is perfect. Call his name and you will find great help there.

At the time Pericles first came to me in this life, I was reading the book *Glory and the Lightning*, and I was absolutely shocked by it. I chided him. You see, I was the one who sailed from Persia, so I had a right to chide him. I said, "Pericles, how could you? How could you be like that? Why can't you be like Count Saint Germaine and Hilarion? In that awful book, that writer says you mixed with those awful people and went to taverns and things." Do you know what he calmly answered me? It's the only time he has ever been very strict with me. He said,

> Those who lived in the world of politics at that time lived among pleasures. Many times would I visit those places if I had to reach those I worked with, but I never walked the devious roads of degeneration that eventually devoured the flame of truth ignited by my virtue and by my love for you. Was not this love of humanity of the highest? And am I a two-sided marble column, one which reflects the light of God and the other which shelters in its shadows the degradation and greed of mankind? I wish you would not think these thoughts, as they are perpetuated by one who reads and writes shallow stories of the times and placed me accordingly with the majority. Was I a part of the majority? Were you? No one knows the truth, that I was truly not part of the statesmen's pleasures. Did they not throw darkness upon both our names? I never ran with a pack of wolves, but I corrected them and used them to achieve my purposes. The columns have fallen now in Greece, but my conviction and laws have changed the lives of men universally. Is this also within the pages of fiction?

I wrote a small tribute to him, very short:

> Pericles, I love you, as I love Skanda, for your worth, your purity, your control, your belief in God and the God in yourself — and for the power to do that which you did so long ago in the Periclean Golden Age and still prove among us now. I love you because you belong to the realm of Zeus, as I belong to Lazumma's line. I love your stature, your courage, your gentleness, your courtesy, your wisdom, your appearance, your uniqueness and your indomitable will. Your patience is beyond compare. Your understanding has made you kind and humble and given you grandeur through these two thousand four hundred years. We are trying to belong to your line of splendor, and we must act accordingly while we are here in the flesh on Earth. To me you are not a man, but a God come down to set men and women free.

Zeus, your son I love, for, Father, he is Thee.

If you will close your eyes, we will end with a trip back to Greece. Go back to ancient Greece now. Close your eyes and take a trip to a time when the Parthenon still stood in splendor. Visualize yourself walking. Still can I hear the sound of our footsteps echoing off the clear pools in the temple gardens, the pools of my memory. These were times when the heavens opened before all of our eyes, and we shared the great bliss of God, right before the eye of God. But now we walk on the paths of righteousness and truth, the saving grace of mankind. Again and again do our eyes and hearts witness explosions of the great glory of that time throughout the heavens, burning like the torches which guard the temple door. Our love for humanity is a silent vigil, a symbol to the universe that the power of love can win.

At this moment I wish to say a little about Lazumma. Where the unmanifest meets the manifest is a being that looks very much like the Statue of Liberty. The person who made it originally must have had a vision of Lazumma. She looks a lot like that statue except that her gown flows like light. She is in the unmanifest and yet she is manifest. At times I've seen her break into a million pieces and shoot out through the universe and draw herself back again. Where we have hearts, she has just a great hole from which this golden substance flows forever out down upon us. Words came from her the other day:

My presence is golden. It flows in the depth of my being, the pristine. It is beholden to no one in all realms, in all beings, in the deepest shadows, for I am not exposed but lie deep as a mystery to unfold. You know me by my presence, but greater depths have I. You speaketh of me as Love, but in reality few can measure my depth. From the most luminous effulgence to the most subtle of patterns do I manifest. My depth knows no bounds, for I am all that you cherish. I am the essence of your own Being.

Inattention diminishes my presence. Lack of attention, lack of concentration puts you at a distance from me. Even the word subtlety does not do me justice, for my essence goes beyond all definition. Clarity invokes me, clarity of being. When the being stands closer, my presence is easily detected. In this clarity, you may perceive more subtle aspects and experience more subtle dimensions than you might even dream possible.

I am boundless. I am closest to that substance which you call God. Infinitely do I flow. Everything which I touch, it becomes of me. It becomes my own substance, my own essence, my own self. In and out of the Absolute flows this substance, for I perpetually stand on the border between the manifest and the unmanifest. All hearts are my reservoir. Can you allow my vastness to expand and overflow, and permanently join my vast ocean of light and love?

Lazumma

Now we will sing a song which came to Larry in an inspiration, for which I thank you, Larry.

Flower in the night, a stand for truth and right,
A Master Soul that takes my heart away.
Perched on high above, hands outstretched with love,
Breathing forth the sacred holy breath.

Lazumma, Lazumma, Lazumma, Lazumma, Aum.

So let our spirits soar, to touch a distant shore,
The rainbow warriors of planet Earth.
A New Age filled with light,
With freedom, love, and right,
Lazumma, fill my night with love.

Lazumma, Lazumma, Lazumma, Lazumma, Aum.[1]

Let that golden light flow down upon you right now. Feel as if the ceiling has opened up and the light is flowing down upon you, covering you, touching your sore points, touching that which needs healing of soul and body and mind. Let the light of God flow upon you now. Flow with the music from the ocean of God. Keep your backs straight and your eyes closed. Fly with the notes to the grandeur of God. Feel the climbing up the hill, making the summit and conquering it. Say, "I will conquer." Feel it.

Climb that mountain. You're getting to the top now. Look down. You see someone below you slipping into the mud. Oh God! Put out your hand and help. Pull them up! Lift them out of the slime and mud! Point out the top of the mountain to them. Take them by the hand.

See the darkness fading from our world and the sun coming up now. We know we're going to make it, for we are the Sons of God and the Daughters of Light. We came on Earth to make it and that we shall do.

Make a vow to yourself that you will march on and march on and march on, and will never stop until you get to the top.

Chapter Six

Imprisoned Glory Released

This is the most important epoch we have ever entered. When the inter-galactic ray came in contact with Mother Earth during the Harmonic Convergence, it was the start of a new evolutionary period of decision and cleansing. How many of you here have gone through a hard time since then? Oh yes, the cleansing is going on. "Oh boy," you think, "what happened? I thought the millennium was coming and what came were all these hardships." It's a quick cleansing, so take it on the chin and accept it and say, "Thank you very much — you're getting me ready and preparing me."

Old friends may move away or turn away from you. They will think you're cuckoo. Let them think so. They'll come back. I tell you, they'll come back. Many will cling to the truth but others will turn and flee from the very truth that would give them freedom from worries and fear. They'll come back. Give them time and space and air so that they can think. Don't hold them. Nobody likes to be pulled by their shirt buttons, right? Let them come. They'll come.

Soon confusion will enter the world in a greater degree. I was rewatching the Nostradamus film. In it Orson Welles says that in May there will be a big earthquake. Whether in Los Angeles, whether in New York, I don't know. Maybe our prayers will protect us and it won't be May. Maybe it will be put back, but he did say May 1988. The Wall Street people are secretly saying they think a crash will come in May. We will not accept any of that. We will pray, and we will get through it. People got through the last depression, and we'll get through this. It means maybe you'll have a little less. Fewer silly things, right?

Soon confusion will enter the world to a greater degree and will try to make you retreat from the very actions which would solidify you into faith and courage at a time when the wonderful new vibration can help you. Be yourself and do not be influenced by any negative person. This is the time for growing closer in harmony, the time of the Harmonic Convergence, to mention again that auspicious moment when Earth's position coincided with the great ray or energy field of the intergalactic force. There were those who went to the Mayan temple for this convergence of harmonic energy. They went out at dark and faced the direction which their compass said was east and stood ready to watch the sun come up. But it didn't come up in front of them, it came up in back of them. The compass was turned backwards as the change in energies came upon the Earth, just as the compass goes off in the Bermuda Triangle due to the continent of Atlantis slowly rising. I often wondered how Cayce's prophecy that the ocean would rise as far as Nebraska would come true. But if Lemuria comes up, you can see that the water that would rise up would move the shoreline back that far. That's when the UFOs will play their part. They will come to give you a chance to be taken off so that you don't go under the water.

On that Harmonic Convergence on the 16th of August, millions or maybe billions all over the world got up at 5:30 a.m. and prayed. I believe that prayers can change destiny. Nostradamus said so and Cayce said so. I think Cayce's dates might have been right originally, but when we read Cayce's predictions we got busy and prayed harder.

This is the time to heave-ho and push with all your might towards God and turn your back on worldliness. Now what is turning your back on worldliness? Does that mean you go into a cave? No! You continue to work, but work for God. Before you go out in the morning, say, "I dedicate this day to Krishna," if you like Krishna, or "I dedicate this day to Jesus," if you like Jesus. "I dedicate this day to the Lord, every moment of it, and whatever comes, I know the Masters are behind it."

Do you think the Masters aren't watching you? A lot of us are vegetarian, but with the heavier vibe that is coming, I say that if you want to eat eggs, if you feel that you need it to hold your vibration, it's all right. You know, I never ask anyone what they eat. I don't care what people eat, but I said to someone, "What did you eat when you were out?" She said, kind of sheepishly, "An omelette." It was the Masters who asked that through me.

Now why did the Masters go to all that trouble? Just to let her know that she is being watched, that they know what she does and therefore she shouldn't sit out there thinking, "I'm eating an omelette — hope nobody finds out." Otherwise the thought goes down into your subconscious and makes you dirty.

You know that old story about when I was in Santa Barbara and staying on a mountain with my friend who was a health food addict. Before, I had been a dancer and had eaten what I wanted. Once I came down into the city, and I went and ordered a thick chocolate malted milk. You would have thought I had ordered a quart of whiskey, the way I sat there. I looked to the left, I looked to the right. I thought, "If they report this to the people with whom I'm living up on that mountain, what will happen?" See, it went into my subconscious and was messing me up. Do you understand? If the Masters hadn't said, "What did you eat?" through me, it would have messed that girl up, messed up her stomach. We have to be free, do you follow me? If you're going to live happy, you have to be free. Therefore, you do that which you feel is right to do, and you do it with glory and wonder and fun. Do everything with an open mind so that you don't hide anything. When the New Age of God comes, you won't be able to hide anything because everybody will know what you're thinking. They'll just look at you and know what you're thinking. So you can't hide anything.

Dedicate all your actions to God. Marry if you wish, but dedicate this ceremony and this kind of life to God. Stay celibate if you wish that path, but turn your whole being to God or you will become desolate instead of enjoying the ecstasy of God inside you. The positive and negative or the male and female energies within us must merge. They become rapturous feelings within you if you are celibate. We become the positive/negative, the male/female within ourselves and stop looking outside. If you choose that life, it is not an easy life. The climb is hard, but when you get up there, the view is great.

God never created man to be in depression or despair. This is a crucial time. You can no longer dilly-dally or be wayward or worldly in your thoughts or actions. You must keep your eyes on the path ahead and walk straight up, not being drawn by the negative to the left or right, but walking the razor's edge path that you've chosen. Somebody will come and say, "Oh, don't be so silly — what are you doing all those exercises for?" Right? Just smile. Don't say anything. Don't argue, but go on with what you are doing.

They used to call me "yogini." I'd smile. Then after awhile they'd say, "She's a yogini" but — aha! — in a different tone of voice after they saw the power of the discipline there. You must follow your own lead from your heart within. Have you got that?

Don't let anyone lead you off the path, not at this time. There is no more time. We haven't got too much time to prepare ourselves, and preparing ourselves means getting right within. What if the UFOs came this moment? How many here are feeling grouchy this moment? One person in the back. Too bad. Then the rest of us will all go up, and one person will be left down here. Maybe we'll grab him and say, "Come on." There isn't any time for that, you see. When they come, they'll say, "Will you go?" You don't say, "Yes, if you take my mother, my grandmother, my aunt, my uncle, my children and everybody." You have to say, "Yes!" And you know they'll take the rest of them. If your kids are at school, they'll go and take them from there. If your husband is at work, they'll take him from there. You just say yes and get on. When you get up there, anything that is happening down here will be blanked out of your mind until the time when you come down.

I saw the New Age of God with the waters receding and the new grass, and I saw hundreds of people from other planets in long gowns and long hair, the Daughters of Light, helping us and showing us what to do on this Earth when we come down again. Sounds crazy, doesn't it, like a crazy fairy story? Really sounds nutty, doesn't it? If I weren't sure of it, I would think I was crazy, to tell the truth.

I'm going to call on Louise. She's got a real whopper of a UFO story. When she was eleven, she lived in South Carolina with her mother. There was a pasture there. She went out to the pasture, and she'll tell you what happened. She was told that she would not remember it until she was grown up. I was sitting with her, taking her back into her childhood, and she was telling me about her childhood. When we got to eleven years of age, she told me this story. It was the first time you remembered it since it happened, wasn't it? So tell it.

It is a little hard for me to remember some of this story since at the time I was remembering it, I wasn't exactly remembering with my conscious mind. I do remember that I went into the backyard. I lived in the country, and there was a barbed wire fence and a pasture with cows. I was standing on the barbed wire fence looking up at the sky.

Up to now, I had always only recalled going out and standing on the fence and being out there a very long time. I didn't ever remember anything else about it, but when Hilda was working with me, all of a sudden everything that happened came back to me.

I was standing there and a UFO came over the pasture. The pasture was very large and the UFO was very large. Actually, it was enormous. It came down about a hundred feet from the ground. I was eleven years old so some of this is really hard for me to recall. One of the things that I do remember is that I wanted them to take me home. It wasn't until I was older that I really ever had an affinity for UFOs. When I saw "Close Encounters of the Third Kind," all of a sudden everything just sort of opened up in me.

I wanted to go home. I wanted them to take me home. They took me up and told me that I could stay for three days. They also told me that when I came back I would not have been gone for three days — I would not have been gone at all as far as anyone else knew. So I went up. I'm very inquisitive and I remember asking a lot of questions. They were talking about coming back to take people and that I would get to come up at another time when I was much older and things were happening on the Earth. I asked a lot of questions about how human beings were going to live if they weren't on the Earth — how we were going to breathe and where we were going to stay and what we were going to eat. In this place where they took me, there was a lot of vegetation, but not trees necessarily. Most of what I remember are giant plants and the sound of dew, as if I were in a sort of rainforest.

I don't know if they told me or if I figured out what would help make the oxygen, where the food would come from, and how we would be able to breathe and get water and everything. There were rooms off behind the vegetation. My understanding was that people would live there. It wasn't like they were bedrooms. It was more as if they were rooms for working and resting and learning for whatever period of time we would be up there. So that satisfied me. I just remember running about and looking at everything and being fascinated by it.

They told me some other things. They told me that they would come to get people and people should go with them, but that I wouldn't have to go on the ship if I didn't want to, that I could stay down here and work. The impression I had was that there would be a great deal of sickness upon the Earth at that time. I just remember thinking, "Everybody is sick. Everybody is sick. Everybody is sick." That was what went through my mind at the time, and that I would be allowed to be down here to help people if I wanted to do that. Because I would be down here for that reason, on a physical level what was happening to everyone else wouldn't happen to me — I would be well. But it would be very difficult to be down here because of everything that would be happening on the Earth at the time. I suppose all the people who decided to stay would have healing power to help the other people who were here. The people who were on the ship would be able to learn all kinds of fascinating things. If they stayed down here, they wouldn't have the opportunity because they would be helping. Not that they would really miss anything, but a lot would be going on in the ship.

I came back and I didn't remember any of this until Hilda took me back in time. It was really fascinating to me, because when I was younger, whenever I was unhappy, I would always tell my mother I wanted to go home. She would tell me, "But you are home," but in my mind that was not home. She used to get very annoyed with me about that.

So now I understand what happened to me and what it meant.

There is another story. The son of someone who comes here was working and a UFO came and stayed all day over the place where he was working. He called the other workers there to come and look at it, and not one could see it except him. All they saw was a cloud. Now you'll say it wasn't there;

it was his fancy. I say they weren't allowed to see it, because they weren't ready to see it. It came down for him, because he had just gone through a real cleansing and had come into a new consciousness. That's the way it is. Those who are ready will see it, and those who aren't won't see it. So get ready. It's never happened on Earth before exactly like this. I mean, it wasn't this crazy when Noah built an ark for a hundred years, and they made fun of him for all that time. For a hundred years he built it — that's a long time to hammer. He finally got it ready and all the people were saying, "Look at that nut, that super-nut. Isn't he crazy? Let's not talk to him. Children, don't go near that place. He's crazy; he's a lunatic." Then the rains came. Ha, ha! The gangplank went up. Those who had made fun of him were on shore, and they went down under. Noah wasn't so crazy, was he? When Sodom and Gomorrah were destroyed, they told Lot's wife, "Don't look back." She looked back and turned into a pillar of salt. These things have happened if our Bible, the Old Testament and the New Testament, is true, which I believe it is. It coincides with the Hopis' beliefs.

The Hopis say they came from the Inner Earth. I used to think it was really nutty to see that little drawing with all of them holding hands and coming out of the Earth. I was the cuckoo one — they weren't cuckoo. I had to grow up and open my mind. Now, my mind is pretty open. I read something and hear it and almost instantly I understand, I don't have to ponder on it. I know that I know that I know that it's right. If you have to ponder a lot with your mind, then you have to get rid of that stupid mind because that will hold you back. We have to come into our heart. That's what we're going to do right now.

Look within. Close your eyes for a moment. Do you hold any grudges against another? We are going to do this twice tonight, now in the Christian way and later in the Jewish way. Do you hold any grudges tonight? Is there anything of that left in you? Look inside. Ask God to reveal it, and if you find a grudge, put your hand up. Please, I beg of you, let God's vibration reveal if that grudge is there. Let His vibration come. Hold that grudge in the light of Christ and let it be dissolved from your consciousness right now. See it bursting into flames. If you have to, light a match and burn it up. Use a blow torch if you have to, but don't use atomic power.

Have you any hatred towards another, deep within, hidden by your external spirituality, hidden by "I've got to be spiritual so I mustn't hate anybody"? Yet down in the memory remains the time long ago when somebody was nasty to you. Your positive thinking and striving could have pushed this hatred or jealousy or greed or any other negation down deeper into the unconscious. If you find any hatred, then let God burn it up. If you have jealousy, look in and see if maybe the person you're jealous of has more problems than you. Have you any greed left or any negation deeper down in the unconscious? See if you have and burn it up! Use any method you want — a match, a flame, or see a light come down from heaven and grab that negation, or a pac-man come and eat it up. Whether it be jealousy, greed or any other anti-God feeling against anyone from this life or whether it be the debris left over from another life, be unafraid to bring it forth this moment to the surface, and ask forgiveness from deep within you. Come from below your rib cage, and ask for forgiveness from the Christ perfection lying deep within you. That light is within you and it wants to shine. Ask for forgiveness, please ask for forgiveness.

If you cannot forgive past deeds or words against you, then this moment ask Jesus, the epitome of forgiveness, to help you. Say, "Jesus, I can't forgive. I can't let go. I can't forgive. Will you do it for me?" As he hung suffering on the cross, he said with deep understanding and compassion, "Forgive them. They know not what they do." Would anyone do bad deeds towards another if they truly knew what they were doing and if they knew that without Christ's grace, the consequent karma of what they did to another would rebound on them? Your bad deeds will only come back to you, so please this moment be free. Know that they know not what they do. Look back and ponder on what you did yourself in your transgressions against the Great Creator.

We must be cleansed and band together in close harmony. I expect this class not to be a class of strangers. There are no "new people," even if they are here for the first time tonight. If you are here, you belong. There must be close harmony, and that is impossible without the grace of cleansing the last remnants of lower self, the self-centered self. The time has come to be free. You cannot draw together in love with the mud of the old self clinging to you. You must be bathed clean in the Christ Light, made whole again as you were in the beginning before we fell from God-consciousness.

This is the wonderful time of Dasara of the Hindus, that is, the nine days celebrating the Mahashakti, or the Great Mother of the Universe. One day when I was in India, I was on my way to see a 160-year-old guru when I looked up and saw way up in the sky in neon lights the number nine. I didn't know what the nine meant. When I got there, he said, "Will you do the nine days of Dasara to the Mother for me?" And he told me how to do it. He told me to get just a few flowers or leaves, to put some butter or ghee in a little dish, make the butter into a little mountain, put a little wick inside, light it, and to sit on the floor and say this mantra. I'll give you the mantra right now: "Eym Hreem Kleem Chamundayay Vijay." Eym means God and hreem kleem are seed sounds, sounds that have not taken form yet. Chamunda is a name of the Mother. Chamunda is like Skanda. Skanda is the one who fights the negative for you, and Chamunda is Durga in her state that also fights the negative for you. Vijay means victory to the Mother to overcome all our obstacles. No matter what Her costume or what Her name, whether She be called Mary, Parvati or Durga, it's only the Mother in a different costume, and if you go high enough, you'll find only Light. The guru said to say the mantra one hundred and eight times every morning. In the beginning, one hundred and eight times sounded like a lot, but pretty soon something happened to me, and I began to have a rhythm come in my body. The rhythm lets the kundalini rise. It gets rid of all the tension. If you are stuck somewhere, the Mother knows how to move you in a circle or forward and back. I did it for the nine days, and at the end on the ninth day I saw this tremendous light — the Mother as the Absolute.

Now I also have to say, Mary to me is Mother and Mary is fantastic. She needs no passport. She can get behind the Iron Curtain. She's over in Yugoslavia. On the television I saw a man who said he was dying of AIDS, that he was in the last stages. He went over to Medjugorje in Yugoslavia, and he's come back in complete remission and gone back to work. He looked very, very healthy. Mary is over there. Mary has been with me all my life. She has been with you, whether you know it or not. I wake up in the middle of the night and I hear, "Silent Night, Holy Night." That's her theme song to me to say, "I'm here. I'm here, daughter." "Oh, Mother, you're here, good." I find myself singing it, "Holy Night."

Let's say three Hail Marys and think of Mary. I want to teach you to use your heart tonight. Don't say: "Hail Mary full of grace the Lord is with thee. Blessed art thou among women and blessed is the fruit of thy womb Jesus. Holy Mary Mother of God pray for us children now and at the hour of our attainment". You see, it has to be "Hail Mary" — ooh — "full of grace, blessed art thou among women, and blessed is the fruit of thy womb, Jesus. Holy Mary, Mother of God" — oh my goodness! You see, by the time you've said one, you're in a thrill. By the time you've said two, you're in ecstasy. By the time you've said the third, you don't know where you are.

It's the same Mother whether it's Chamunda, whether it's Mary, whether it's Parvati. Maybe you won't like that, but we're all made of the One Essence of God and take different forms. If I wear velvet today and a sari next week, it's still plain old Hilda, huh?

It is also the Jewish New Year, and it will soon be Yom Kippur. So let us get a head start on Yom Kippur, shall we, and be pathmakers for the others. We will have a short meditation on cleansing in the Jewish way. Let's do it in honor of the Jewish New Year. Let's throw out the old and resolve to change.

The wrongs held within hurt no one but yourself, for they backfire into the memory bank. That is a perfect name, for it is a bank filled not with material wealth but with memories good and bad which remain there until they arise and either bless you or curse you with their vibratory rate. With that in mind, let us at this holy time become one with the sacred God-given Jewish tradition by looking into ourselves and asking forgiveness for wrongs done unknowingly or knowingly.

Close your eyes. Sit straight. Really mean it. Now imagine yourself before a body of water. Stand high on Mount Sinai and in your mind create an ocean below you. Feel like you have an old dark velvet robe on you, heavy or maybe even dusty. Let us have faith that God can and will forgive our sins as we bring them forth with a deep penetrating desire to be like our Creator. Let us have faith that by so doing we can go back into that original consciousness which is happiness, divinity, which is free from the inner deep remorse which dams the free flow of light through our temples, the bodies. Oh, you're getting somewhere now, kids.

In imagination, take the end of a ball of white thread. Ask to remember from the subconscious any wrong you have done this year. It's this year we have to cleanse. Think back to when you talked back to somebody and said, "Oh, shut up," when you could have talked nicely and said, "Oh, would you be quiet?" Think how you could have changed your ways this year and not been so stupid, not been so worldly. Now wind the thread into a ball. Take any thought that comes to you of what you've done wrong, and wind it in. Use your hands to do it if it helps you. Wind it in, wind it in, wind it in. As you wind in the dirt of the past, the thread will turn black. Come on, get busy. Come on, wind it in, wind it in. Find anything you've done wrong this year. Oh, now we've all done things wrong. We didn't hold the consciousness of God every moment of every minute of every hour of every day. Of course we didn't. We didn't remember who we were every moment of every day. We forgot and said, "I'm sick. I feel rotten." That's a blasphemy to the God within. Come on, roll it in, roll it in. Now when you get a good big ball of it, take it and throw it into the ocean. Come on, throw it when you're ready. Throw it away from you. Throw it with your hand into the ocean. Do it. Take some action. Actually throw it. Harder. That one only went over the cliff. Into the water, come on, throw it.

Now take another lot of thread and find something else you did wrong this year. Don't demean yourself with unworthiness. Just say, "I'm getting rid of it." That's what this Yom Kippur is all about. Go on rolling it in. Have some fun. Come on, be kids. That's it, good. When you get a ball of darkness, throw it over the cliff, into the water and out of your consciousness. Now have a look at your dark robe and see what's happening. The dark robe you have created in the past twelve months is getting lighter and lighter. See it getting lighter. Come on, use your imagination. Look and see if there is anything left. Ask God to reveal anything. Say, "God, will you reveal any deed that I've forgotten that needs cleansing?" Ask, really ask, come on. Be with me on this, kids. Now look at your robe.

Now feel the gentle breeze of the golden light of the Holy Spirit coming over you. Come on. Feel it on that inner plane as you stand on Mount Sinai with your arms out, waiting for the Messiah. Let the Holy Spirit blow you clean. Say, "Blow me clean. Blow through me." And the robe of darkness has become a robe of shining white. That's what it says in the Bible. There will be people whose robes will become white. See your shining white robe. Stand there, glorious. Believe in yourself. Believe in the God within you. Believe that you're free. *Sh'ma Yisroel Adonai Elohenu Adonai Echad.*[1] Rejoice!

While we are in this mood, let us ask pardon from God for the wrongs done to this world. As we are now free from our own transgressions, we have a right to ask. Feel it with me this moment.

We ask You, God, forgiveness for those of the white race for their treatment of the Native Americans, the Indians. Please let us ask forgiveness. They starved them. They gave them blankets with smallpox germs on them. They lied to them. God, forgive the white race for their treatment of their brothers, the Native Americans. Mean it in your heart so God can hear it. It's not for me to ask, but for all of us.

God, we ask forgiveness for the people of this planet for the treatment of our Jewish brothers and sisters in Europe during the Hitler regime. We ask forgiveness, God. We ask forgiveness, and we give forgiveness.

Forgive the white people for the slavery of the Africans, who have not yet taken their rightful place, but will in this age to come. Forgive us for we knew not what we did.

God, forgive us for the treatment we have given our lesser brothers and sisters, the animals. We know what we do and yet we do it. Please forgive us.

Forgive us, Mother Earth, for our horrible treatment of your body — the waters, your veins of gold, the minerals and coal that we have pulled out of you, not even asking permission. Please give us, your children, a second chance to redeem ourselves, Mother Earth. We've spoiled your water; we've spoiled your air; we've spoiled your earth. Now we're asking for a second chance. Let the power generated and left for us on Earth through Moses, Jeremiah, King David, beloved Jesus, the saints and Masters of Wisdom and the Brothers and Sisters of Light keep us safe and free from harm in these ensuing years.

Before Jesus went on the cross, rams and lambs were slaughtered. He went on and let himself be slaughtered so that this New Age of God, this Golden Age, could come in and our sins could be forgiven. If we believe, no matter how bad we've been in any life, no matter what we've done, if we believe that he did sacrifice himself like a ram on the altar, then we can be forgiven and God can do it for us. Amen.

Let's sing "Alleluia, Alleluia." Rejoice that you're free. Rejoice that you're free and have been forgiven. We are free! Raise your hands in freedom and believe. Angels, hear us. Oh, yes, we are free!

I want to talk tonight about our human realities and God's reality. Do you know what I'm talking about? Your reality is, "Oh, I've got to go to work in the morning." "Oh, that boss is so rotten." "That lover is letting me down. I think he's two-timing me." "That girl, I don't really believe in her." "Oh, will I lose my job?" This is humans' reality. What is God's reality? God's reality is, "I created everyone perfect in this world and they are still perfect, but they are imprisoned. The glory is imprisoned within them." Imprisoned within them — did you hear it? Deep down in there you put some bars, and you put a key, and you imprisoned the glory of yourself inside yourself with your human reality.

Along with this goes the thought, "What is this to thee? Follow thou Me." I get through reading an awful thing in the newspaper and I say, "What's this to me?" I have to read the newspaper, because I have to know what's happening. I have to know when Wall Street is going up and when it's going down, so I can tell you. When to move out of the city, when not to move out of the city. When to stop the classes and when to have the classes. You understand? I have to keep track of it. Oh, there was a time in my life when I didn't have to do that because I didn't have any people around me. I was a loner, so I could just think of God all the time. I didn't have to think of this Earth because I didn't have any responsibilities. Unfortunately the Masters gave me some responsibilities, and they got bigger and bigger and bigger. They started with one person in my home and then two and then three and then my room filled up. We moved to the front room, and then we moved to somebody else's home, and then we moved to Saint Luke's, and then Dean Morton said, "Would you like to come up here to the Cathedral?" I was ready to quit by then, but I said, "Well, I guess God has spoken," so we came up here. So when you read the newspaper, read it and then say, "What is that to me? I follow Thee, Lord. I follow Thee, God. What is that to me?" Learn to say that.

The whole world is our own self. Within us is the macrocosm and microcosm. Let us come down from that Absolute for a few minutes and look around and see a world outside ourselves. If we look carefully enough, we will observe that all we see is what we have at sometime gone through, perhaps in a little different form, disguised until we scrutinize ourselves carefully. You might look at someone and say, "He's a drunk. He takes dope." Then you look inside yourself and you say, "Well, what do I do? Maybe I put on the TV or I go to a show so that I won't have to think — the same thing the drunk and the addict are doing." So it's ourselves out there, but in a different form. You're not drinking, you're not taking dope, but you're doing something. Maybe you're having a malted milk shake, like I did to forget that health addict place up there, to give myself some ease. But that is just the same, don't you understand? So you have to look into yourself when you look out to the world.

When somebody comes and tells you a story that is identical to your experience, you are free if you no longer react to it and can just listen and observe and say, "Wow, I am free — there's my subconscious out there." But you have to observe it without reaction. Observe it like that and you are free. Yes, come out of your subconscious and see it outside, and it will never be in you again. So when someone comes and tells you a story, be very patient. Listen to it and say, "Wow, that's my own self of the past." Be unafraid to look at it. Perhaps it's in a little different form. It is disguised until we scrutinize it carefully and see the same vibrations in the other person's story. Their actions, though different from ours, have the identical meaning of our own experience. The whole world is within ourselves. We are doubly burdened by our own reality of the world — the reality we feel deep within our being — and the so-called reality we see outside. You see, that reality that we see inside makes the outside world even worse. Our true reality that we know is there makes this outside reality more miserable for us.

I will discuss for a few moments the reality we create in our mind in our little world. We make our thoughts, feelings and actions the reality of our lives. In the Golden Age we're entering, you won't have to say anything. You just think, and anything you think is made. Whether it be food, whether it be this, whether it be that, you have it. Even in this life now, if you will live that way, you will find every thought that you think manifests — boom! And you say, "Wow!" Manifestation is instant. You can have it now. You don't have to wait until the Golden Age comes because the Golden Age is within you.

Are you all so submerged in your little worlds that you have blinders on and do not see the glory of others? Each of us sees a situation differently, depending on where we are on the spiritual path. Some smolder in their version of the reality of life and lose the glory all around them. Youngsters have their own reality, especially those in their teens and up a bit in years. What they are able to conceive of and think in their short sojourn on Earth, that's all they know.

I wrote to Sai Baba and I said, "You're wonderful. Your message is glorious. You've come on Earth to teach us, but nobody's living it, darn it. They live it with their heads, but not their hearts." I haven't heard from him, but I don't think he's mad at me, because I love him and I wasn't telling him anything he didn't know. I was just confirming it.

Those in their teens are all going to college and they think it's so important, but how are they going to use it? I don't know. It'll be a new world, not even the same kind of bodies, in the sense that these bodies will take on immortality then. What does that mean? It means the atoms in you will be alive and vital, and those moments you have in meditation now will be what you experience all the time. I'm going to show you later tonight how to do it.

We can see the doughnut or the hole in any situation. Saint Therese always saw the doughnut. Others see the hole. If they gave her a cracked pitcher, she said, "Oh, thank God, I don't have to worry about it any more." Others would say, "Look at what they gave me back — a cracked pitcher." Ramakrishna had a new shawl and it dragged in the earth, and somebody came up and said, "Master, your new shawl is dragging in the dirt." He said, "Oh!" He threw it on the ground and stamped on it and said, "Now it's all right," and put it on again. He didn't have to worry about it. That's the doughnut and not the hole. The other one saw that this new thing was getting dirty, and somebody who had given it to him would get mad that he wasn't treating the gift in the right way.

Every day in the paper we see the tragedies. Whole lives are spoiled due to people's misconstrued conceptions of what those around have done to them. Two wonderful boys from high school got into an argument. One took out a knife and stabbed the other one. One has his life ruined, and the other one is dead and has gone to paradise. Over what? Because somebody said something rude to a girl. There's something wrong, do you understand? There is no self-control. It's a wrong world. That's not the world to live in. That person could have gotten up and said, "That wasn't nice to do. Would you please apologize to this girl immediately?" Most likely the boy would have, and then he would be alive and the other one wouldn't be in prison. We must control ourselves and come into a new way of living. Some grow up and see clearly; some never grow up.

That is the tragedy of life on this Earth planet. Not a nice planet, to say the least, but it could be if the inhabitants — and that's us — would come into a mature consciousness of the one reality: that God is real and you are real, and all that exists is the reality of God; that you are perfect, and you are not sick; that all are created perfect in His image and likeness, equal, loving, kind. How glorious! How wonderful this world would be if we were to overlook that which seems evident and see the reality of life in all life — especially in our fellow being. On other planets, all are of the same temperament and development. On planet Earth, there is a mixture of analytical creatures called humans and a few real human beings of love and purity. People of the mind analyze everything, analyze their neighbor — all wrong.

Can't you understand and see we can no longer live in the muck and dishonesty of our own limited reality, but must conform to the one reality of the Creator? To obey God will bring you into a wonderful ecstasy and joy and wonder. It makes Mother Earth and the Masters very happy and makes the angels dance and sing with joy.

I want to do an experiment tonight. Do you mind Darryl coming up here? I'm going to show you something, and you're all going to do it. This is the way to work — silently. I'm going to talk to him and tell him all the glorious things about him, but I'm not going to say it with words. My guru, Nity-ananda, never talked to me with words, just with the head. You have to have a feeling with the head and the heart and below the heart, the emotions. I'm going to talk to him silently, and you see if you can feel it. Let's see if he can feel it.

Do you feel it? What do you feel?

> "Very spontaneously a smile rose up in me, and it just
> smiled out into the whole world, and I felt like I was alive
> with joy."

Did any of you feel it out there? If two can do it, how about all of us doing it and exploding the world? Now what did I say to him? I said to him, "Darryl, you are so wonderful. You love God so much. You don't care about money. You are so wonderful. God loves you so much. Skanda loves you. You are so beautiful and so kind and so good." That's what I said in my mind to him and look what happened to the air with just two people.

Now, let's see what's going to happen with all of you. Think on someone. Even if you really hate that person, tell them how wonderful they are, but don't talk with your mouth. Don't say it out loud. Look straight ahead. Think from deep within you. Down below the rib cage feel what you're saying. Feel what you're thinking. I want the air to change in here. It hasn't changed yet. Go on. Love. Feel. Think of all the beautiful God things you can say to them.

Oh, now it's happening. I'm beginning to see smiles come on faces. Oh, it's beginning to happen. This is the Golden Age coming right now. This is the way you're going to feel in the Golden Age. This is just a little tiny replica of it. Come on. Oh, tell them some more things. Tell them how godly they are. Bring forth the glory in them, the perfection in them. Oh, come on, I'm feeling it. I'm feeling it.

Oh angels, come down and see what's happening in our room here.

Masters, come and see what's happening to your children here. They are seeing the perfection in each other.

Just sit and enjoy. Accept the glory. Tell the person you're thinking of about the perfection inside them. Tell them that the glory's inside. Tell them they're God's children, that God loves them and that you love them. Oh, it's wonderful, it's marvelous, it's glorious, it's divine, it's God. It's the Golden Age come into this room. Shambala. Go on, we don't want to stop. We don't have to say it out loud. I'll tell you how wonderful you are while you are telling them. Down below the rib cage, let the love come in. Feelings — not head, but heart.

Truth is within ourselves. It doesn't rise up from outward things. Whatever you may believe, there is an inmost center in all of us. Find that center now in yourself. Now that you've got that peace, find it in yourself, a center inside you that has been activated tonight, a center where truth abides in fullness. Feel it inside yourself. Find it. Find the imprisoned glory and take the key of love and open it up with that golden key. Open it up, my darlings, come on, open it up.

Don't be imprisoned any more. God is inside you. "The gross flesh hems in this perfect clear perception which is truth. A baffling and perverting carnal mesh binds it and makes all error. To consistently know the truth opens out a way whence the imprisoned splendor may escape." Let it escape in this room. Angels, come and take of it, and take it to those who are ill.

I say this moment, "I am that I am. I am that I am. I am that I am." Say it with me this moment; think with me this moment as I say, "I cannot have any pains in me because God has no pains. I am in His image and likeness; therefore, I can have no pain." If you came with pain, get rid of it right this moment. "I can have no sickness for God has no sickness and I am in His image and likeness. I cannot have AIDS because God has no AIDS and I am in His image and likeness. I cannot have any cancer because God has no cancer and I am in His image and likeness. God has no cancer or else the whole world would scream. I have no despair because God has no despair. I am in His image and likeness, therefore, I have no despair. I felt what love was; I felt myself tonight. I know myself for what I am."

Find the real nature behind the physical appearance of everybody, and do that for anybody. When you are sitting in a room, you can tell everybody silently how wonderful they are, and they will respond because the God in them and the God in you know each other. The God in the dog and the God in us know each other. The God in the fly and the God in us know each other. The God in the snake and the God in us know each other. I've told you about the time when I walked out on a mountainous path and there was a rattlesnake ready to strike, but it didn't strike because I had been loving snakes and seeing the God in them. I loved that snake so much it responded and didn't strike at me.

The easier it becomes for us to go beyond conventional boundaries and conditions and move in understanding, the more harmony there will be with all life on this planet. Meister Eckhart said, "When I preached I said, and I regard it well said, that not a man in the world can conceive with all his learning, with all his education, with all his college and his degrees that God is in the very meanest creatures of this Earth, even in a fly."

We must not say words, but feel words. They are cups in which God's essence is held, and the essence of God is in them.

We're going home now. The peace of God be with you. The love of God be with you.

Chapter Seven

The Power of Grace

I'm going to introduce you just very slightly to somebody called Hildegard, if you don't know her — Saint Hildegard of Bingen. Living and dying almost nine hundred years ago in lush and beautiful Bavaria, she was a poetess, abbess, musician, artist, healer, scientist, theologian, prophet and mystic par excellence.

Now what she said — it could have been written today for us. She believed that true sin represents a rupture in the cosmos. We have a rupture in the cosmos right now, up in the sky. And who made it? We did. God didn't make it. We have ruptures in our relationships. Do you have any ruptures in your relationships? If you have, get them back together. If I think I have anyone that's mad at me, I telephone them. I want to be right with everyone. I don't want any ruptures in my relationships. You do the same.

She wrote: "Now in the people that were meant to be green and vital with aliveness, there is no more life of any kind. There is only shrivelled barrenness. The winds are burdened by the utterly awful stink of evil, selfish goings-on. Thunderstorms menace."[1] Couldn't that be written for us at this time? She was a prophetess — like Nostradamus, she foresaw what was coming: "The air belches out the filthy uncleanliness of the peoples. There pours forth an unnatural, a loathsome darkness, that withers the green, and wizens the fruit that was to serve as food for the people. Sometimes this layer of air is full, full of a fog that is a source of many destructive and barren creatures, that destroy and damage the earth, rendering it incapable of sustaining humanity."[2]

Hildegard regards the ultimate sin to be ecological: a sin against the earth, against the air, against the waters, against all God's creation. For in injuring God's interdependent balance, we are destroying all life, including our own.

I want you now to close your eyes and visualize the perfect world, the way you would like it to be when all this illusion is finished. When the mudslides have gone and the earthquakes are over, what is going to be left? Visualize it in the most imaginative way. Einstein says, "Imagination is more important than knowledge." We create with our imaginations. This group here could create the new world in the ethers right now.

Want it with all your hearts. Create it this moment in your hearts. Want it more than breathing. Want it more than anything. We want it for our children and our children's children, for generations to come. We want a new world, kids.

Thank you. Your thoughts have gone out and created it on the upper plane. We have only to bring it down here now.

I have a lesson that the Masters woke me up at 4 a.m. to write. They give us the usual warnings. I'm sure we don't need much warning, what with the earthquakes and the stock market.[3] I think by now we have the picture of what's coming, and I feel that we don't have very long to get ready. Daniel talked about it thousands of years ago. Jesus talked about it two thousand years ago. And I've been talking about it for twenty years. We aren't ready yet and we don't have very much time left before changes will come. We'll like those changes because they'll bring what we want on Earth.

The Masters gave me that day a wonderful ending of hope and told me how to instruct you to get the unworthiness out of you. They said, "As the times get more perverse and the sun seems no longer to shine in our lives, that is the moment to cling to God and accelerate our yearning for our Creator." That is the time, Nostradamus told me, you have to think about God. That is the time, the Mother told me, you have to think about the Mother. You don't look left or right at that time. These are times of tests and decisions. With the Harmonic Convergence came also the time of decision: shall I go back to the worldly ways or shall I make the steep climb to God? Am I attached to the old world? Does it still pull me?" These are the questions to ask yourself.

Saint Hildegard saw that evil stealthily stalks the streets. See, kids, you can learn by grace or you can learn by experience. One of our girls went walking by herself at 10:30 at night on the boardwalk down at the New

Jersey shore, and of course she got beaten up. I have warned you to use your intuition and your senses and not to do stupid things any more. We will think about her tonight with love.

It was unnecessary. Do you understand? You have to use your intuition and listen — "Should I be here or should I not be here? Should I walk down this street or should I walk down that street?"

In all walks of life, I see destiny being worked out before my eyes. I turn the television on and I see destiny being worked out. A young boy walks down the street and for no reason at all someone shoots him. You say, "Isn't that terrible?" But in some other life, he must have shot someone and the debt is getting paid off. Do you understand this? But if he had listened to his inner self and the voice said, "Don't go down that street," he wouldn't have had to pay that karma because he would have been in God-consciousness instead of personality consciousness. Karma doesn't have to come upon you. It can be wiped out if you turn to God-consciousness.

Yet I see those I love choosing the lesser path of travail rather than the more austere path of God, which finally leads to satisfaction, bliss and joy.

The Masters say, "Children of God, have you not suffered enough under the spell of evil which often comes in the many guises of education, intellect, modern living, wrong careers, fear of changing old antiquated concepts? Look what you as humans have done to our world, the only world you know, through looseness and not adhering to the laws sent down to us by our Creator through our forefathers."

We have suffered through ignorance generation after generation, far too long accepting life's patterns of decay. Isn't it time we stood up and said, "No! No!"? If you see something wrong on the TV, turn the TV off! Say, "No! What is that to me? I follow Thee, Lord!" After you read something in the paper, you say, "What is that to me? I follow Thee." What is it to us? It is nothing to us, this world. This is a dream world, a school. We are at the lowest ebb thus far and should not go farther into the mire and muck of earthliness. We should turn about and put a halt to the old and say, "This far and no farther."

Was it not enough to see Lemuria sink into the sea through our iniquities? We all must have been there. Was it not enough to hear the screams and experience the horrors of Atlantis as it crumbled into the ocean and was lost from sight? Was it not enough to hear the rumble of Pompeii and then be frozen in fear? What more havoc do we want to cause upon this one-time

Garden of Eden? How much longer will you fall under the Adamic Law, Adam's law? Adam fell, not into a fig leaf, kids. He fell in consciousness, into self-consciousness. We, as his children, ever since have been in self-consciousness instead of God-consciousness, and we're wending our way back to God-consciousness. Do you understand this clearly? Jesus went on the cross to break that law that had come in when Adam fell. Did not Jesus pay the price on the altar of love to break this evil law for us? Did he not bring love in, love for God the Father? He said, "I and the Father are one."

Will you not come into this realm of love, come out of the old and into the new? Jesus said, "I come to give you a life more abundant." Yes, more abundant, even in the midst of the chaos upon this Earth, even in the midst of the poverty and mire and mud.

You can live in the world or you can live above it. It depends on which way you want to walk. You can't straddle the path. You can't walk the path of Mammon and God, too. You have to walk the one path, two inches off the ground. You have to pull yourself two inches up above everything and say, "What is this to me?"

How much longer will the Mother of the Universe, the progenitor of us all, allow Her children to suffer the Hitlers? Must there be more Holocausts to bring us to our senses? Cannot a few come forth and lead the way out of the dark forest of despair?

Master Hilarion has said, "If seven on this Earth could harmonize, the world would be saved." Just seven. Where are they, those willing to give up self-consciousness for God-consciousness? I haven't found seven, I'm sorry to say. There's always something. My students may love me, but when it comes to loving each other, there's criticism in the way. Even if they don't say it with their mouths, they're thinking it. Your thinking is as bad as your saying, do you understand? We proved that one night here when we all silently sent good thoughts to each other and we all felt it. I'm not saying you should be like nuns or monks or yogis — they quarrel, too, amongst themselves and within themselves. I know, because I stayed mostly in convents when I danced overseas, and I didn't find the harmony there that should be within a group. I don't find the harmony anywhere one hundred percent, I am sorry to say. Sure, you love me and I love you. You can look in someone's eyes and say they're an angel. But if they burn the food, will they still be an angel to you? If they leave the door open, let the dog out, leave the toothpaste top off and the cockroaches come, are they still angels?

Or do you start criticizing them with your mind? Oh, you think, I mustn't speak evil about them, but I can think it. So where are the seven?

When I see a person turn from the pathway or the laws of God, it is like holding a person's hand who has slipped overboard. The hand slips away and you see them sink into the dark waters. My heart cries; my heart is saddened. God gave us choice, and our choice has been wrong.

Wars have hardened our hearts to evil, haven't they? The news on the TV has made us callous, for we get hardened. Do you understand that? You see a body on the TV, a shooting going on, a train wreck, a plane blowing up, and you pull yourself in and you get hardened to it. You have to.

Corruption looks us in the face left and right. Many are the good souls who have lost their way. Are we to condone this life of evil? Are the signs of herpes, AIDS, earthquakes, mudslides, and economic changes ravaging our world not enough to turn us back and make us cry, "This far, no farther"?

Let us put a stop to all this before it is too late. Let us all, however many hundred are here, make that vow this night. I'm going to ask you to make that vow to your own soul.

I came to Earth, as did you at this time, to help, to be stalwart, to teach others steadfastness. Cannot we dedicate our lives this night to Earth's redemption before it is too late? For time is running out. The signs are all around us. Soon, I must leave this city. If you would take time, you would see the handwriting on the wall. If you could be allowed to see the hell worlds that I have been shown and have entered into to save souls, you would shudder with fear.

This is a mighty time of decision and a time to choose. Your right path is at hand. You must choose wisely. If you're still halfway in the world and halfway for God, then for God's sake, make a stand for God with all your heart tonight. You can still go out and work, you can still marry, you can still have your children, you can still do everything you ever did, but who's first? God Almighty! Let's hear it! God! God is first!

If our brothers of the skies could come so far from other planets to warn us and promise us succor, should we not listen? Are we so dense we cannot or will not hear? Never in the history of this planet has there been a time like this. Yet we go on our so-called merry worldly way, which deceives and leaves us desolate in the end.

The very Gods themselves have come to Earth to encourage us, Gods like

Skanda, who is here tonight. I can hear him saying, "Skanda! Skanda! Skanda!" The Sons of God walked the Earth at one time. If we live right and put Mother Earth together again, they will again walk beside us — the Gods, the Masters and all the beloved ones.

Mary says, "I send out a plea to your souls and to the souls of every man, woman and child on Earth to turn about and acknowledge the sacrifice of my son, Jesus, as the lamb sacrificed on the altar. He has already broken the satanic powers, if you will but turn your life about and accept the way of Light. It is hard to go against the crowd walking downhill to its destruction, but you must."

I personally remember long ago, kids — it's an old story — when I got off the ferryboat in San Francisco at 5 p.m. Thousands of people were coming out of their offices after work and walking down Market Street to the ferry. I was the one person walking uphill. I was being bumped and knocked, and I had to push against the masses spewing out of their offices. That was the first time I ever heard the heavens speak. Master Hilarion spoke thus: "From this day onward, daughter, you will walk against the crowd." It has been so, but so many of you have joined the upward climb now. We are all here at last, walking in the right direction.

With all the signs around us, I cannot understand why anyone would go with the crowd. With AIDS so virulent — and all who can read between the lines know it will annihilate our race if it is not checked and a cure found — how can a person still go the way of loose-living sexual habits, knowing that the Antichrist is already on the job, planning — planning stealthily and insidiously our destruction? How can we turn back to this world once we have experienced even a glimpse of God's light or the Universal Mother's love? We must turn our backs on the world and not be a part of it, walking in the midst of it untouched.

God sent us down to be a part of this Earth, to experience it. I'm going to tell you why you had to come down and walk among those on the Earth. How would you have compassion if you didn't walk among those on Earth and know what it was all about? How would you know what pain was if you didn't have pain sometimes? When you have said, "I have pain and I'm ill," would I have known what you meant if I had just lived in a cave? We have to come into this Earth experience to understand each other that way.

We know right from wrong and always have. You've always known right from wrong, haven't you? In the sixties, didn't you know that deep inside yourself somewhere was a voice saying, "This isn't the right path." True or false? Of course, you knew that deep inside yourself while you went your merry way. We know right from wrong and always have, if we look back into our lives. Otherwise, why would we lie when we do wrong to cover up, and by so doing uphold the wrong?

Oh, how to get to the heads and hearts of people and wake them up! I call out to you in desperation, but it is not you I need to call to, for you have seen and felt a touch of the Light. It is those who have not been given a chance to know the Light whom we call and go out and help, is it not? Is that not what you're doing? If you aren't, do it from this day onward. Make the opportunities.

I will answer a couple of letters. A girl here in the class wrote to me and asked, "Does God forgive?" Of course He does. He does not judge us. You, by the laws set down in ages past, judge yourself. Turn about and face the light of God's glory, and there you will feel your Creator within you. Whom would God love the most and embrace and respond to the greatest? Those already in the Light or the one who has the courage to come back home after experiencing a life of sinning? Which would God choose, do you think? The sinner, of course. The one coming home would be welcomed with open arms.

Of course, God forgives, but you don't forgive yourselves. You're so dumb! Start being knowledgeable tonight and forgive yourselves. This night, you're going to.

Of course God forgives. He forgives. He forgives, but first you must acknowledge that you have strayed. Ah, yes, you have to acknowledge that you strayed from the faith, from the path of God, that you left the Light and that you now feel remorse within. Feel remorse within and then God will welcome you home. He holds no judgment, nor does the Mother. She only wants Her children of the Earth to come into the warmth of Her arms, Her loving arms.

The Masters told me one time to leave home. My brother was an alcoholic and was drinking heavily. He had not come into his realization of God and was angry with me for my belief in God. Now with whom did my mother choose to stay? She adored me. I adored her. I asked her, "Come with me, Mother." Did she come with me or choose my brother? What do you think? She chose my brother. She said, "Hilda, I must stay with your brother. He needs me. He needs me the most." That is the way of the Divine Mother also. That is the way of God, too. So whoever wrote me that letter, know that God forgives and never did have anything against you. He never judges, but calls you to come out from the masses who are walking the wrong way down the hill to sorrow and suffering.

Another in this class wrote to me, "Why did I have to suffer this sickness?" This age upon Earth now is a cleansing time. Think of your ills as cleansing opportunities if they persist when you tenaciously know the truth of yourself. If you know the truth of yourself, which I'll help you with in a few moments, and your ills persist, then it's a cleansing for you. It's getting rid of your past and preparing you for the New Age of God. Use it to learn patience. A miracle is an instantaneous change. A healing can take time and teaches patience, kindness and gratefulness; it changes separateness into oneness with others, for others come to help you. Do you understand that clearly? It can be a spiritual boon.

Don't hold onto your feelings of unworthiness. Great hardships and glories are ahead of us. Come into the heart and come home. Does not the song say, "Just as I am, I come to Thee, Lord, just as I am"? We come just as we are. If you think you have to spend the next few years cleaning yourself up, then you're wrong. You come just as you are and God does the rest.

Tonight I'm going to call the Spirit down, if It will come, to flow over us and heal us, to get rid of unworthiness and make us clean.

If you only knew, kids, that up there no one has judged us — we have been judging ourselves. Did Saint Therese ever come to me and say, "Have you been baptized? Are you a Catholic?" Did Mary ever say to me, "Are you a Catholic?" when she came to me? Did Jesus ever say, "Have you been saved?" No! They don't judge up there. They just come and love. The angels come and look at us and they see us moaning and groaning down here and trying to clean ourselves up. We must stop cleaning ourselves up and let Him clean us up. Do you understand this?

Now I want you to close your eyes just for a moment and I want you to understand that you've never been judged. No angel has judged you. No God has judged you. No Lords of Karma have judged you. You have judged yourselves because inside you the little voice said, "This is not right." Or you've been told, "This is sin" and "This is right."

This moment, will you be freed? If they don't judge us up there, those glorious beings, why do we judge ourselves then? They look down at us — I was joking at home about how we go into the bathroom and take off our clothes and think no one is looking, when really there's no ceiling on the bathroom and they're all looking down at us. That's just very silly, but it gives the idea. The world up there is looking down at us, waiting for the light to come over us. And they never judge. Why do we judge ourselves, kids? Why? Please give up your judgment of yourself. Give up your feelings of unworthiness. This moment find anything that you thought was sinful and say, "They never judged me and I'm not going to judge myself, because if I do, I'll judge somebody else and I don't want to. I understand what sin is now and can be more compassionate in this world and be more useful to God." Please free yourself this moment if you've been harsh with anyone. Nobody has judged you.

The only thing I would ask is that tonight you go into your room and say to God, "I did this and I did that and I did this and I did that and would You redeem me?" To redeem is to take back. "Will You take me back? I was a darn fool. I made a lot of mistakes." But this is a school down here, and sometimes you don't pass your tests.

I see someone crying this moment. If you think you've sinned, just ask forgiveness and then forget it, and don't go and sin any more. That's what Jesus said: "Sin no more." Don't make mistakes any more. We haven't got time. We're here to help others. Tonight go into your room and say, "I did this, God, I did that, I did this" — all the things you've never admitted you did wrong. You always upheld yourself. You said, "I didn't cause that trouble. Somebody else caused that trouble." Go in and say, "I did cause it. I caused it, God. I caused it, and I'm so sorry, God! I'm Your daughter, I'm Your son, I'm so sorry. Will You take me home? Take me home. Because You don't judge." He doesn't forgive because there's nothing to forgive.

Does He not say, "Come unto Me, all ye who are heavily laden"? If you're heavily laden this moment, put your burdens at the feet of the Lord. Place them there and leave them there and don't take them up again.

I don't want any feelings of unworthiness in this class again. All of your experiences have been lessons only — you have been learning how to walk upon Earth. Many here are from other planets and many are very high souls that don't come often to this Earth. They don't know what this Earth is all about and they get entangled with it. But once we've gotten entangled, we see our mistake and we just step out. There's not one person in the heaven worlds who blames you or looks down on you or curses you, and, therefore, you will not do that to yourself from this day onward.

Those who are heavily laden, place your burdens at his feet, those sacred feet bludgeoned for us so that we could be turned toward a new direction and a life abundant — abundant in love, loving just for love's sake.

Feel this moment that you don't need anyone or anything to love. You just are love. Feel love this moment. Work for the sake of working for God, live your life for the sake of freedom.

Let us turn our backs on the ways of Adam. That was when we as a race became self-conscious, egocentric, personality-conscious. Let us take our rightful place on the planet Earth as God-conscious beings this moment. All have the same reality: we are made in the image and likeness of God and deep inside have never left that consciousness. Know it this moment. Say, "God, I'm in Your image and likeness." Say it inside yourself dozens of times now. "God, I'm in Your image and likeness. God, I'm in Your image and likeness and, therefore, I am perfect." Look inside, chip off that clay and find the golden Buddha inside you. Find the golden Self inside you.

Look inside. "I am in God's image and likeness. God is not sick and I cannot be sick. God is not fearful and I cannot be fearful. God is not without money and I cannot be without money. Oh, God, You are so wonderful! And I am in Your image and likeness." Believe it this moment. Say it as I say it. Say it and believe it, because it's true. Anything else is a lie. It is true. All have the same reality — that we are made in the image and likeness of God and deep inside have never left that consciousness. It has all been a nightmare, a terrible dream. Let us awaken and know help is at hand. The climb is steep, but the rewards are great, the air fresh and rare. He has trod the path ahead of us and so we cannot go astray or get lost.

I am beginning to feel the Holy Spirit come now, before I ask for It. When Jesus left this Earth, not through death but by rising above the density of the Earth, he sent the Holy Spirit to comfort us until he returned. This is the dispensation of Jesus. He shall come again with Moses and Elijah by his side. Those who would like to make a commitment to their own soul's perfection and be bathed in the light of the Holy Spirit will have an opportunity tonight. Prepare yourself inwardly while I chant sounds from the ocean of God.

Open Your heavens, God, for these children. Open Your heavens for them and pour down Your Spirit, and let them know who they are. Let them walk out tonight with their backs straight, their heads held high, and know they are children of the Most High.

Rise with the sounds. Come into your forehead and rise into the joy, into the light. Let your burdens drop off, for you are children of God, my beloved children, my beloved children. Shambala! Shambala!

I ask for the Holy Spirit. Those who would like to make a stand for their own souls can come forward. You don't all have to. As we sing "Amazing Grace," don't get up until you know that you have to, and then stand that God may look down upon you and say, "This is one of mine!" Oh, God! "One of mine!" Don't stand or come forward until you feel it. Those sitting, pray for the others. We're going to make a commitment to our own souls now, to the light within ourselves.

I ask that the heavens open and the Holy Spirit flow down upon us. Let it flow down, please. God, don't let us down. Let it flow upon us.

May the holy angels fly around this room and bless each one of you. May Ammal bless you. May Mary bless you. Inside yourself say, "I make a commitment to my own soul, the beauty of myself, to live to my highest, for I am a child of God." Oh, yes. You are a child of God. You are. Oh, God! Oh, God! Ask for the blessings to come upon you and upon everyone in this room. May it be from the upper chamber that the holy light flows down. May it come through the top of your head down into your body. Just believe, believe, believe, believe, believe. If you're sitting, pray hard for the others. If anyone speaks in tongues, speak out. Don't hold back. If any word comes to you, call it out. Share. Don't hold back, kids. This is one time when you can give. Shambala. This moment ask for forgiveness — don't wait until you go home tonight. If you've done anything you didn't like, say, "God, forgive me this moment and wipe me clean. I'm going out of here clean. I'm going out new. I don't have to go home to my room and ask for redemption. I can get it right now." Right now. Right now. Feel the joy of it. Feel the love of it.

I thank you for making it beautiful. I thank you for your souls. I thank you for being you. I thank you for coming here. I thank you just because you are you. If only you could see yourselves as I see you — so beautiful, so perfect, so divine, wanting God deep inside you.

Chapter Eight

The Hereafter Revealed

With Thanksgiving so close at hand, I tried to think what subject would be the most appropriate. So tonight I will take up two themes: Thanksgiving, which we will take up at the end, and Paradise, our "Home, Sweet Home." We will give thanks for our lives on Earth and find out the truth about life after passing over, so we can give thanks for that also. I will talk on life in Heaven and life on Earth — in other words, everlasting life.

Let us now draw away the curtain between the so-called two worlds, this little curtain that has been there hiding the other world. I don't want to make this world on the other side so wonderful that you will all want to go. I'm giving a fair warning — if you take your own time to go and not God's time, you are going to land in a dark space over there and wait out the time that is written in your palm. In other words, if anyone commits suicide, that person has to wait over there, sitting in a dark space doing nothing, twiddling his fingers and waiting for the next fifty years, until he catches up with the time allotted him.

We come onto the stage of life as little babies, and we make our exit on the other side of the stage when our part of the play is finished. Then why the hullabaloo? Why the hysterics? Why the holding on to our beloveds? We know when we leave heaven and come down here to this school, the acting school down here, that we have to leave and go home someday. Yet, when somebody wants to go home who is about a hundred and five, you hang onto them and ask me to pray to keep them here.

In the Orient, I once saw a little baby a few weeks old pass on — the only person I've ever seen pass on. I was called in to try and heal it. It had been given so many intravenous injections, there wasn't a vein left to penetrate. I called in a friend of mine, a Christian Science healer. She had started to pray and know the truth when she suddenly saw a tall, handsome young man in a long white robe on the other plane. It is very unusual for that to happen to a Christian Scientist. This beautiful spiritual person reprimanded her in no uncertain terms and said to her, "Leave my fettle alone," rebuking her as if she were interfering in his territory of choice. The term "fettle" means flesh or body. The little child, the vehicle that soul was going to use to be on Earth, passed on, and there was the usual grief and crying.

This brings me to a book I wish everyone could read and therefore be more cognizant regarding the afterlife. The book I am referring to is called *After the Change Called Death.*[1] It tells about a lady who had two children, two boys, and they both passed over at a very early age, when they were babies. She herself passed over after a long life, when she was elderly, but she had always mourned the two little babies and had often called their names while crying with grief at her so-called loss. After she passed to the other side of the thin curtain we call death, two beautiful male figures appeared to her. As these two male figures came to her, they said, "Our mother!" They told her they were her two sons whom she had thought lost. They said, "You never called us that we did not come. And we spoke to you and tried to comfort you, but you did not always hear us..." She was so filled with foolish grief, she could not feel, see, or hear them. They could not penetrate her negative feelings and make their presence known and so comfort her. Do you understand that? Somebody's going, "Ohhh, they're gone," but they're still here, so full of light, trying to say, "Be happy, be happy." What a mess we are down here. Why aren't we intelligent? Let's get intelligent tonight.

This book costs very little and should be in the hands of everyone to lend to others. We must abort our ignorance and know what heaven and afterlife is all about.

What we call life is really but one experience in a continuous everlasting life in many different worlds. In our dreams we go into subtle worlds which are the worlds people inhabit when they pass over. I am aware of these worlds. The Masters have taught me to go into these worlds. Often you call up and say, "Oh, I saw you in my dreams, Hilda," and I say, "Yes, I'm busy at nighttime." You understand? The Masters have taught me to go into these places, and many of you also are doing the same thing to help up there.

Some of you are aware that you are helping at nighttime. I am very well aware of these worlds and can say that this book gives a correct picture of the ordinary person's life after death. By ordinary I mean the usual person on Earth who lives without much thought of God and the path.

If you are a soul bent on mastery, you would proceed differently on the other side. You would dwell among perfected beings and have a chance to continue to learn the lessons of living. The perfected beings would teach you and train you to be leaders of humans. They would watch over you on that plane as they do already on this one, guide you, and love you. You would not seek out your immediate family when you went over, though you would contact them in love if you wished. This is because you realize that each time on Earth you have a different mother, father, brother, sister. You are helped with guidance from the Masters and choose before you're born in each life those who will further your advancement and at the same time give you a chance to help others. You choose, but sometimes while you are on Earth you don't think it's the best. You don't think you chose the best mothers, and the mothers don't think they chose the best children either. But they did.

The heaven worlds are the reality. Down here is just a school, a place for educational processes, a learning university where you get grades, though you know it not. Few have a clear concept of the other worlds or the many mansions referred to by Jesus. That is why I take up the theme of paradise that is in this book. After my long years of experience of helping on the other planes, I can readily endorse this book for you. As I've said, it gives a clear picture of afterlife.

I would like to explain a little of the advent of this book. A spiritual woman passed over, a high soul, and had a great desire to communicate to let others down here know what it was all about. She wanted to clarify that there is nothing to fear for your loved ones who have passed on or, should we say, passed out of your vision. They will meet you again with joyous rapture. She was freed from the limitation of the physical body, yet she had an identical body, only younger, up there — a body freed from all the pain, disease and old age she had when she left. How many have seen me on the inner plane? I'm very young, usually wear blue, right? Vivacious, stern, loving, but young.

Reading from the cover of the book: "Mrs. E.B. Duffy, the writer of the book, was suddenly connected with a spirit which had made the transition to the other side and has written down, like a secretary, what she had heard." Linda Shore, who comes to this class, brought the book to me which her father, Mr. Frank Shore, has printed and made possible for the public to obtain. He is Jewish, and it's a very unusual book, I think, for a Jewish man to put out about the hereafter. His group in Florida, Life Forces Research Foundation, is the motivating force behind this book. He, like myself, believes that in these trying times, when so many loved ones are passing on, we should be educated and more acquainted with the process that takes place.

Wouldn't you like to know what happens? I think that it's a great adventure. When I was over in India, my mother just appeared to me — she was in America — and she said, "I'm sick; I want to go on." So I sat down and wrote her a love letter. I said, "Do you want to go on to your great adventure? You let me go on my great adventure to India, so I'll let you go on your great adventure, if you want to go." I released her, because it is a great adventure.

We need to be educated on the subject called life. We study so much at school, at universities, and get degrees. But if I ask most people what they think heaven is like, or what the other side of the curtain is like, there is some insipid, vague answer. "It is peace." "It is light." Or, as we were told at Sunday school, "Everyone plays the harp." What a future to look forward to — eternally playing a harp! Oh my God! Imagine, to just sit there and play a harp all the time! Right. Especially if you can't play it. There is no concrete idea of the great adventure everyone has to undertake. You all undertook an adventure to come down here. You went before a board and said, "Hey, I want to go down there," and they asked, "Why do you want to go down there? What are you going to do?" Then you said, "Well, I want to help those people. They're a mess down there. I want to help them!" So they said, "All right, go down, but be sure you don't become a mess yourself when you get there." But we forgot that part. We all became messes. Well, I can't put everybody in that category, just most of us.

The planes or mansions or worlds I speak of tonight are for the beautiful people who down here have lived a regular life of struggle and conquering, or paying off karma and sometimes making more karma. I am not speaking of saints, perfected yogis, Masters, or spiritual giants, of which there are few, but of the run-of-the-mill, regular kind of striving people who are doing their best to pass their test in a chaotic world school. There are many who start their day with love and fill it with love and then end it with jitters after a grueling eight hours of work. Yes, you start your day with love: "Oh yes, today is going to be wonderful. I dedicate it to Krishna, to Jesus and Mary." As the day winds on, you keep saying, "Yes, I'm dedicating it, I'm dedicating it." By the end of the day, your body is going, "Arrrrr, let me get home. Look at this subway!" You've lost it!

The person telling her story in this book who had passed over says, "In looking back from where I now stand, I cannot but wonder that the earth-life assumed such importance."[2] Oh, everything is important to earth-life, isn't it? What are some things that are important to you? Getting a husband, getting a spiritual wife, getting a star child to come down, paying the rent: all these become epic to you down here. Do you understand me? I'm making this humorous tonight because life is humorous. I hope you all have fun with this story I'm telling tonight.

She couldn't understand when she got up there and looked down, down here, why she had allowed everything to assume such importance. Now take something in as I talk and say to yourself, "I'm not going to let this world be so important to me any more.I'm not going to get upset when all the dishes break, and the stove is on and burns everything. I am not going to get upset when my husband comes in and says, 'What's that smell again? Burned food?'" You are going to say, "Yes, darling" and smile a beautiful smile at him and run up and throw your arms around him and say, "You've got a dopey wife, darling," and he'll agree. Didn't Jesus say, "What is that to thee? Follow thou Me." Jesus tried to teach us of the shallowness down here.

Someone asked me what happens to all those who pass on during the Tribulation. There are only a few, you know, a few who are going to make it from there into the New Age of God. What is going to happen to the rest of them? Well, they will all go home like all students at the end of a term.

Mr. Frank Shore gave me permission to read some passages from the book, and I'm going to do it. So we're going to have a book review now, but you still have to buy the book.

I love this part. It refers to all of us. She's gone over and she says:

> I lived, I toiled, I suffered, I loved, I struggled with
> temptations, and I sometimes sinned — the common lot of
> humanity. In these words may be summed up not only my
> earthly existence, but that of most mortals. For those to

whom any of these experiences are not given in the earth
life, they are reserved in full measure in the life into which
I have now entered.

So you can't beat it. Now this is the part I love.

As I had all my life fought and struggled, and sought to
attain the unattainable, so, true to my nature, I would not
even allow myself to die in peace, but all unwittingly
prolonged and postponed the hour.

All of us try to postpone the hour for our beloveds. People call me on the
phone and say, "Pray for so-and-so, pray for them." We postpone the hour
until we finally see them in agony and we give up, and then they give up.
What happens? Listen to what happens.

At last I became wearied, and fell into a sweet sleep, a
sleep so restful that in the half-consciousness which pre-
ceded the moment of complete unconsciousness, I remembered that in all my life I had experienced but one or two
as perfect and satisfying. For such a sleep I was contented
even to postpone the hour of death. When I awoke it was
with that almost guilty sense of one who feels that he has
slept longer than custom or prejudice sanctions; and for
the instant I was glad that I was very ill, that such an
indiscretion might be forgiven me. The waking was even
sweeter than the sleeping. I did not care to open my eyes,
but I lay filled with a sense of peace and rest such as in the
long, weary years of my life I had dreamed of and longed
for, but never before experienced. How sweet was the rest,
how perfect the peace! If only it might endure forever! But
I was better. I was not to die after all, and I must presently
submit to the old bondage, and again know the weariness
and unquiet of life. Presently I became aware that there was
a sound of subdued voices in conversation in an adjoining
room. Though I could hear them plainly through the open
door, at first I gathered no sense of what they were saying;
and then as I became more fully awake, I heard a sentence
which fixed my attention in an idle way: "I have no doubt
she meant well; but, then, she was so very peculiar." The
response came: "Yes, very; and very set in her ways." Again

the first speaker: "She saw a great deal of trouble, but I have no doubt she brought much of it on herself. You almost always find that that is the case." "That is so. Why I know ———," and then followed a grotesquely distorted narration of certain incidents in my own life. I was startled.

Now if anybody's lying there looking like they're sleeping and they've gone on, and you've gone to see them to say good-bye, don't talk about them, because they are going to hear you. You got it? They're going to hear you. If you want them to know something, tell them something nice, but don't go behind their back and talk. Always when they are in the coffin, they are there — beside it, not in it. Everybody goes and looks down in the coffin. Why don't they look next to the coffin, and look at them? I rarely go to funerals, because sometimes the one who passed on follows me home. But when Rudi passed on, that holy man Rudi, I went to his funeral. I was sitting in the front seat, and there was a little space next to me. Rudi was a pretty big guy. He came over and wanted to sit next to me. So I pushed the man next to me over, and the man looked at me and wondered what the Sam Hill I was doing, making a space there and pushing him over so Rudi could sit down. He couldn't see Rudi like I could.

Of whom were they speaking? Of me — me? "She was?" What did it all mean? Did they really think me dead? With a guilty conscience of having played eavesdropper, I hastened to call one of the speakers by name, to assure her that I was still in the land of the living. They were both neighbors, and I knew them well. She paid no heed to my voice, and the conversation went on without interruption. Again I spoke louder than before, and still they heeded not. I was now aroused to the fullest mental activity, and utterly forgetful of my supposed enfeebled condition...

For an instant I seemed frozen with terror...

— because she looked at her own body —

...My God! was I then really dead? How can I describe to you the emotion which swept through me...

I could not silence those babbling women, and so I let them talk, and for the first time in my existence, had an opportunity to see myself as others see me. Well, the lesson was a good one, and not without its uses, even though I had passed beyond the influences and conditions of the earth. It held up an imperfect mirror before my spiritual vision in which my defects of character were brought into greater prominence by distortion; and thus the first lesson was imparted to me.

Are you understanding this? There was a group of three there: one who could hear them, and two who couldn't hear her. She said:

We were a group of three, although one was invisible to the other two. As they were unconscious of my presence, so I soon forgot theirs, while I looked with a strange wonder upon the form of that which had once been I.

That reminds me to tell a story again. Harry doesn't mind me telling it, and his wife would not mind me telling it because I loved her. I went to Harry's wife's funeral at the Greek Orthodox church, and I came in just a little late, so I was just following the bier in. I sat down, and his wife came and stood by me and didn't go down to the front. I said, "You must go down there." She said, "You think I'm going down there? That's not me down there. Here I am!" She stood right beside me the whole time. When everybody went down to look at her before they closed the coffin, I said, "You'd better go down there and give them a blessing." She said, "I'm not going down there! That's not me!" I said, "Well, why don't you go and sit with your husband then?" She said, "He's talking too much. He can't hear me because he's saying, 'O beloved, I love you so much. O beloved, I will miss you so much.'" He was so busy talking to her he didn't wait to hear what she had to say.

Am I making it clear and humorous at the same time? We've all gone through it thousands of times, kids. You've had so many incarnations and have been through it. There was one very strange case I heard a man tell about at a lecture. This is a true story. He passed on, and they covered him up. Then he woke up, and he thought that he would go and get a cup of coffee. He didn't know he had passed on, so he just got out of that bed and went down the hall. He went to the coffee shop, and he said, "I want a cup of coffee," but nobody answered him. He kept on saying, "I'd like a cup of coffee, please." Then he tried to find his way back to the room, and he'd forgotten the number of the room. He finally found the room, and he was covered up. In the morning he came alive again, really alive on this plane, and he woke up in the morgue and was able to tell this story. God let him experience this and tell us the story so we would know what it was like first hand. That's a true story, a very famous story, in fact, and I met that man.

The woman in the book says:

> Then I was dead! How strange it seemed to be dead, and yet with such superabundant life! How mortals misapprehend the meaning of the word. To be dead means to be alive with a vitality earthly humanity does not know...I had fallen asleep on earth; I had awakened in the land of spirits...I found myself upon a great plain which gently inclined toward a valley...

All her life she had wanted to be on this plane. Do you remember I told you one time that I complained to the Masters and I said, "I work all day — I answer the phone, I do healing. When I go on the inner plane I work all the time. When do I get even a moment's rest?" So that night they let me go to a place like this plane, a very sweeping plain down to a lovely stream. On the other side was a gate. On that side were the dead people. On this side were the living people, only they were in the dream world. Do you understand the difference? The difference between death and living is that while living there is a silver cord attached to your umbilicus that connects you with your earthly body. When you go up at nighttime, if a noise comes in your room, on that lovely silver cord you come swishing in. Have you ever come in upside down because you came in so fast? That's because you didn't come in slowly down the chute-the-chute. That's the only difference.

There is a person named Margaret in the book who is a guide up there. Margaret brought her one day to a woman who was in despair. It seems this woman's husband had nagged her, been mean to her all the time, been jealous of her and had given her a terrible life. He had passed on. When she got over there she had it in her mind that she should go and see her husband.

> The woman looked up inquiringly. "You are thinking of the man who was once your husband," Margaret continued..."When you are ready to go to him, not with a revived earthly love, but in a spirit of heavenly love, which is ready to forgive and to aid, then you will see [him]...Have no fears,... there are no fetters here to bind the soul...."
>
> "Are there, then, no husbands and wives — no marriages in this world?" I asked earnestly.

"In heaven they neither marry nor are given in marriage,
but are as the angels."

That's what Jesus said when he was asked, "If a woman has many husbands, which one will she live with up there in heaven?" He said, "None." None because there are no husbands and wives up there.

My mother and dad were the cutest couple you've ever seen. He was in real estate. They would walk down the street hand in hand, come home to lunch hands swinging, and go out again swinging hands. They were in love. They were romantic. They were darling. Everyone in the neighborhood adored them. I saw Mother after she and Dad had passed on. I said, "Mother, do you ever see Dad up there?" — this person that she had walked her whole life with. She said, "Well, sometimes in passing." You understand? Does it make Jesus' answer a little more vital?

Then, in the book, they go to a place that looked like a library. It was a kind of temple. This lady said,

"Do they, then, have public libraries here?"...

"You mistake; this is a library of record, wherein all may read, whenever they choose, that which pertains to the lives of themselves and others. Here are the true biographies of earth, not the false, superficial affairs which pass under the name in the life from which you have come."

She opened a volume...

I've seen those volumes and volumes and volumes, shelf after shelf of our lives, what we've done. She read about her husband in there, that he had been like he was because of the genes he'd inherited from his parents and grandparents.

"Take me to him! Take me to him!" she cried. She seemed to feel that every delaying moment was a reproach until she should stand face to face with him.

They went down and down and down, from this light, glorious place where she was, into a dark, dark, dark place. Margaret spoke to the wife.

"My child, do not reproach yourself unjustly....Blame not yourself, but rather the unjust human law and popular sentiment which refuse to allow those to separate whom God hath not joined together."

In other words, she lived with him a whole life of unhappiness. Margaret said that the laws of the Earth had kept them together. It would have been better in her case if she had lived her own life, and he his.

> We had passed out into a barren plane, and the path was rough and stony. The sky, too...seemed to become gradually overcast, until...there was scarcely more than twilight..."Shall we go back?" Margaret asked. "Oh, no, no!" the woman responded..."Oh, I pity him, so deeply!" she exclaimed, "but there is not one throb of love for him in my heart."

The man was in a dark, dank place. I've seen these places of the hopeless, mean people. We make our own world there. We make our own hell. No, God didn't make any hell for us. What we are and what we think, that is our world when we pass on. So be sure you are making a wonderful world for yourself and helping your mothers and fathers to be joyous and happy so that they too can have a wonderful world. Don't annoy them.

Then he saw her. So this man who had passed on said,

> "You have come at last!...I have been waiting for you day by day ever since I heard you had entered spirit-life; waiting in this solitude until I thought I should go mad; and yet you never came! You saw everyone else, of course, before you thought of me!"

The same old guy, he hadn't changed! Going over didn't change him. He took himself with him. Doesn't it make you want to be better? We'll think about this before we close tonight.

> The old repellent feelings seemed to be struggling to come back in the breast of my friend. I whispered to her: "Remember the record."...[Then Margaret said,] "We must remain here no longer."...[The man asked,] "You will take me with you?"...

Now listen to what happens when they take him. This is what happened to this man.

> He entreated so pitifully, that his wife seemed to know not what to say. She looked inquiringly to Margaret.
>
> "Let him come, if he wishes," she responded...
>
> So with a cheerfulness he had not yet manifested, he walked beside us, forgetting his past grievances in a flow of jubilantly happy conversation.
>
> As we returned, the sky gradually grew brighter and the

air purer until we had nearly reached our starting point. The man had hesitated more than once on the route, apparently stumbling oftener as the obstacles in the path decreased.

Did you hear that?

"I can go no further," he said..."We must stop here. I cannot breathe, and the light almost blinds me. We must retrace our steps a little way, for this climate is certainly not a healthy one."

He couldn't take it, do you understand? They had to leave him there until such time as he would all at once make an effort in his soul and say, "God, will somebody help me?" Then will come down those great workers, those angels, and lift him.

It reminds me of a Sai Baba story. The fisherwomen carry fish on their head and go around saying, "Mahla! Mahla!" When they go past you, how those dead fish smell! But they're used to it. This fisherwoman was put in a palace, and there were flowers and orchids and daisies, flowers everywhere, and she said, "What is this awful smell?" So she went out and slept with her fish. Do you understand? We like what we are used to.

My brother was an alcoholic and when I came back from India, I didn't know he had passed on — they forgot to tell me a little incident like that, you know. So I said to my other brother, "Where can I see Walter?" His face fell, and he said, "He died three years ago." But I didn't let that faze me. I went to look for him on the inner plane, and I found him. He had been an alcoholic, and he was tied, just sitting tied in despair. I went with all my love and my light, and as I went near him, I didn't even have to speak. I saw him rise up and go up into the heaven world.

That is the work we can do. We are not to criticize a drunk. We are not to criticize a person on drugs. We are to send our light and lift them. This is our work, for all of us that are here. We are workers for God. So this lady learned how to work for God on the inner plane.

In the book, another lady passes on. They take her to many places up there, but she keeps looking for her idea of heaven. She asks about harps, so they bring her a harp and she is surprised she can't play it. She keeps asking for Jesus, thinking if Jesus is not there, it can't be heaven. They had told her at her church that she would have everlasting life with Jesus Christ so she continued in fear, blind to the light that was there. What could they say? "In my Father's house are many mansions." If you want to be with Jesus Christ, you've got to go to the highest mansion there is in the ceiling of God. I asked a doctor who passed over, "Did you see Jesus?" because I knew he was Catholic. He said, "Yes, passing I saw him." That doesn't mean we are not going to be with Jesus. Jesus is teaching us what to do and how to live to make this Earth a wonderful place. Jesus is darn busy, isn't he? Can he sit in one heaven and just administer to only a few people? Just one group? No! He's ministering to all of us everywhere at the same time. What is he doing? He is teaching us how to become what he was — the Christ within us. So if you have that Christ within you when you get up there, of course you'll see the Masters.

I will diverge from this book now. Somebody has asked, what is the relationship between Jesus and the UFOs. Where does Jesus come in? This is his dispensation and the UFOs have come down to help his dispensation. Sometimes you'll go onto one of the planes of the Intergalactic Council, and you will see Jesus there. Everything is one that's working for good. Are you following that? There is no separation of God.

I'll close this off with just a little bit of the glory of it. Two people went over. They were both elderly, both stooped and tottering. One remained like that. He found himself with the infirmity of age still clinging to him, his mental power still weakened and his spirit come to a halt, as it were, in progress. Blind to the beauties which surrounded him, he said that this could not be heaven because this was not as he had pictured heaven to be. The other man, equally feeble physically when he passed over from the Earth, quickly lost the traces of age upon his entrance into the spirit land. His form speedily appeared erect, his step fine. He was in his true self immediately.

Sometimes it takes some time, if a person hasn't been taught, to let the transition go on. Sometimes it takes ages and ages. In the case of my father, who was agnostic, he had to wait five years on the inner plane, and then he appeared to me. He had died at about sixty, but when he appeared to me, he was twenty-three years of age. Mother, who had been two years older than Dad and had always hated it — she always lied about her age, you know (Oh Mother, please forgive me) — she also looked twenty-three. She made up for it on the inner plane.

Have you gained anything from tonight? Have you gained something by knowing what it's like over there? You make your own world, whatever world you make here. Say you've longed for a house, a perfect house. When you get there, that house will be waiting for you. But that's if you have willpower. That's if you develop will here. If you have inertia and are namby-pamby, and you say, "I'm going to meditate next week or maybe in six months I'll meditate, after I get through with this job," you'll try to manifest something there and it will be only half manifest. Is that clear to you? You make your own hell and your own heaven on the other plane. There are no angels up there condemning you. There are no saints up there condemning you. Jesus is not condemning you. God is not condemning us. We condemn ourselves, and so when we get there we haven't made a good place up there. Have you got it clear? I think everybody here has made a good place, but I don't want you to go too soon.

So I want you to sing, "Row, row, row your boat gently up the stream/ Merrily, merrily, merrily, merrily, life is but a dream." What is it? A dream! Life is but a dream! Have you got it clear? Let's make a good dream, shall we? Let's make a really wonderful dream down here. Let's say, "The heck with the Tribulation. We're going to be up here in spirit now and not wait until heaven." We're going to bring heaven down here.

As they think and create up there, do we not think and create down here? Have you not noticed that you create down here? Have you not noticed that you think of somebody, and then you walk down the street and you see them? Have you not thought of something or read about something and then you see it on every billboard? Do we not create down here? But it's a little slower. Some people go on moaning about their ill health from the time they're young and say, "I'm sick. I'm sick. Oh, I feel so rotten." "How are you today, Maggie?" "Oh, I'm not good today. This is a bad day. It rained and the winds came." They're fine now, but wait fifty years and they will have manifested all they talked about.

So what have you been talking about? Be careful. Every word that you talk goes out in the ethers. They say someday we'll be able to "pull in" the words of Jesus, "pull in" the words of Moses, "pull in" the words of Gautama Buddha. I hope they don't pull in our words.

We have talked about passing through to the other side and going home. Now let us talk about healing so we can linger on in the school down here and perhaps take a postgraduate course in the art of living to its fullest and most abundant. To be abundant and healthy one must be holistic. What does holistic mean? Let us examine it together. Of course you know, but let us think about it. To the Masters in the Hierarchy, it means being completely integrated, all bodies working together — that is, the mental, the physical, the emotional and the soul-self, all in coordination.

How many have run home and come back since you've been here — in your thought form, in your mental body? Put your hands high. Let's see how many left me. Uh huh. How many got gebobbled emotionally with the stuff I said? Hmm. You see, you're not holistic.

We should be thinking, feeling, acting as one. Then our soul can come forward. Sometimes our mental body is in complete control because we have studied with that teacher and this one and have been to all the workshops and the lectures. Yes, we are controlled because we know we must not and cannot be negative. We are controlled. Oh yes, we have to be controlled; we can't say anything negative. That was the first lesson taught us. Yes, we have physical control because we have studied hatha yoga, yoga positions, raja yoga. But oh, that iceberg that is hidden under all this. In an iceberg, two-thirds is hidden underneath the waters, which represent emotions, and one third is above. Oh, those emotions!

During the war, a friend of mine, Jan, was on watch in the trenches. There were guards stationed at four posts. The guard at the second post would go down and go to the first post, and then the one at the third post would go to the second post, and the guard at the fourth post would go to the third post, and the guard at the first post would go to the fourth post — to make sure they weren't sleeping, you understand? This friend of mine was kind of psychic. One night he saw this guard coming. It was raining. When the guard came to a puddle, he disappeared in the rain. Five minutes later he saw the man coming down the stairs again. What was happening the first time? Yes, thoughts, the mental body. The man over there was most likely smoking a cigarette and said, "Oh heck, I've got to go over in that rain now," so his mental thought came ahead and then disappeared. Then five minutes later he got up and came. Complete uncontrol. Instead of saying, "I'm comfortable here," he could have said, "Now I get up and go." That is being holistic. Clear?

When I went to Sivananda's ashram — oh, I was young and ardent — I got up at 4:30 a.m. in the dark and went up to the place where they do yoga. Oh, I was all full of life to find God — by standing on my head. I got there and I sat down, and I heard two yogis talking. One yogi had a little handkerchief on — he'd given up everything except the handkerchief. The other one also had given up everything except the handkerchief he wore. To my horror, one was saying, "You can't do a headstand on my pillow." The other one said, "Yes, I will." The first one said, "No, you won't." They went on like this — in the yoga camp of Sivananda! I was completely devastated that they had given up everything except a pillow. What are our pillows? You have to think about what your pillows are, kids.

When I was at Nityananda's, I went out into the woods — again ardent, ready to find God at any moment. I walked out in the dark and went into the pools there. One pool is so hot it practically bakes you; you come out red like you're half cooked. From there I went out in the forest, and I found this tree where Nityananda used to sit. I went and sat under it, and I thought, "This will surely make it for me." I was sitting there in a wonderful position, when I heard footsteps coming along through the grass and the leaves, and I heard an angry voice say, "You can't sit here under this tree." I opened my eyes and asked, "Why not?" There were thousands of trees there. It was a forest. It was a jungle. He said, "Because it's my tree."

So I learned early to say, "Yes sir, yes sir." I said, "Okay," and he said, "Go and find another tree." I said, "Yes, thank you." That's why I get on in New York City now. When somebody says, "That's my parking place," I say, "Oh, yes, sir, have it please." You have to learn to give in. Doesn't the Bible say, "Resist not thine adversary, lest he rend thee"? I felt like that guy was going to rend me with a knock on the head. He had given up everything, except a tree. If he had been spiritual, he would have looked at me there and gone under another tree.

Can you find in yourself anything of self-preservation? Maybe we're carrying a lot of packages, and there is a small package and a big package. You have a backache, so you say, "I think I'll carry the small package, because I have a backache. I'll let him carry the big package." That's self-preservation — instead of taking a big deep breath and saying, "I'll take the big one, thank you" and trusting that God will take care of your back. What self-preservation have you got inside you? Oh, subway seats! I can talk about that because when I used to ride the subways during what I call the "crush hour," the doors would open and wooooooh, everybody would go in. I'd stand back. Not because I thought I'd get a seat, but I just stood back. Every time I did that, when I walked on, there would be a seat for me to sit in that somebody hadn't seen. It wasn't because I was an old lady, because I was younger then. It works, kids.

In the caveman days we needed that self-preservation as a weapon. We needed to have that — what do you call it — adrenalin. "Whoa! What is that sound? Who is that coming at us? Roll a big rock in front of the cave! I just got a whole big animal in here, and they'll come and take some of it." We don't need that anymore, because we've got God. We don't need that "whooooof" anymore. We need to be free and easy and trust the Lord and get rid of that self-preservation.

Let's look into the subtlety of it. If we have wiped out unworthiness through God, now let us wipe out this last vestige of ego right this moment. Close your eyes for a moment, just in the position you're in, whatever uncomfortable position you're in.

Ego brings discord, sickness and all kinds of mental ills and physical ills, not to mention emotional ills. It means we don't depend on God to give us our daily needs. If we try to hold on to ourselves and our needs, it doesn't work. It takes faith to stand back, and know there's a seat on the subway or a bus, when everybody is pushing to get a place.

God will provide. "Seek ye first the kingdom and all shall be added" is a reality, not a dream. I want you to come through these times ahead. Since the Harmonic Convergence it has been very hard, hasn't it, my beloveds? It has been tough. It is a time of decision. You have to make decisions about what to do: whether to stay in New York City or whether to get out of New York City; whether to go to Boulder, Colorado or not. There are always decisions you have to make now, and you have to make them with your intuition. I am giving you tuition out here, but you have a better teacher inside you which is called intuition — the teacher within you. That one will never send you wrong, if you will listen to it.

In that book I talked about earlier there is a part that I missed where the lady who has passed on looks down on a circle, a spiritual circle. She said she saw four of her old companions down there sitting in a seance. She saw all these spirits around, all ready to grab on to them. One lady was kind of a "whoop-de-do" lady, so when the spirits spoke they gave her that kind of talk. Another person had her own ideas, and a Master trying to push through an idea into her mind couldn't get it into her mind because she was too shallow. Another person sitting there was a very high soul. She seemed to have a force field around her, so no lesser entities could get near her, and therefore the one who spoke to her was the Great Master or the Divinity.

We have to be sure our intuition is not being fed by lesser outside influences of the world. You may be sitting at home, and you're feeling wonderful, and all at once you feel irritable. You say, "Where did my mind go?" Then you say, "Oh, it went to so-and-so who's having trouble." If you're not wise, you'll say, "I am irritable" instead of saying, "Let me send a blessing to that person who made me irritable."

Keep a force field around you at all times from now on. Stand firm and keep it in front of you and in back of you, to the left and to the right and above you, covering you above. Stand in that force field and walk this Earth. Then there will be no tribulation for you at all. Do you understand this clearly? This is what I come here and talk for.

On a different subject, a young man called me and said I had come in his dream and touched his hand. He asked me if there were others present in the dream and wanted to know what else I had said in the dream. I was noncommittal, for so many of you were there where I touched his hand on the inner plane, the dream world.

What I have to say now, I say unto all and not only to him. I shall repeat what I said to him on the inner plane and to you. I woke up saying it to you, many of you who were there, and the words were ringing onto this plane as I came in. This is what I said.

In the morning you go to the bathroom to wash your teeth or whatever you do, and you look at a mirror. I want you to look in that mirror and use it as a means of obtaining health and positivity. It is a simple thing I'm giving you. When you get up in the morning, see yourself well in the mirror. Go beyond limitation. Say: "Every day in every way I'm getting better and better. Every day in every way I'm getting more beautiful. Every day in every way I'm getting more abundant." Just look in the mirror and don't look at the self you see, but say, "Oh, am I beautiful! Oh, I am so healthy. I am so abundant. I have everything in the world. Everything is wonderful." And you will create it. As on the inner plane, you will create it on this heavy plane down here.

I saw a man on the TV who had AIDS. He looked wonderful. He said to everybody, "Look at me. I have kept my mind positive. I go to the mirror, and every morning I say to myself how wonderful I look." He said the doctors told him he was terminal four years ago, ready to die. He said, "Look at me. I may still have AIDS, but look at me. My friend, who has had AIDS for six years, is even better than I am." This man looked handsome, wonderful and healthy, because he was not going to the mirror and saying, "Oh, my God, I'm dying of this. I'm dying of that. Oh, my God, I feel so rotten this morning. Look at my face; look at the wrinkles. Look at — oh, my God." No! You don't look at it. You go to the mirror and you say, "I am so beautiful. I am so divine. I am so perfect." Let's say it. "I am so abundant. I am so perfect. I am so glorious. I am so radiant. I am so beautiful. I am so abundant."

Maybe you think this is too trite. Maybe you think this is too nothing. Well, then, why are you always moaning? Groaning and moaning, huh? Don't groan or moan anymore. We don't want any "groany-moanies" around here. You're going to look every morning in the mirror. How many will do that? All right. How many won't do it? Is there anybody who doesn't have a mirror?

Now we're going to have a little prayer for Thanksgiving. Think of how many things you are thankful for. I'm going to say a few things myself. Then you give thanks inside. Please start with the people that were mean to you and give thanks for them, because those are the ones who have made you strong and have given you muscles.

Let us go deep within our hearts in gratitude for life. O God, thank You for letting me come down to Earth and meet so many friends, and also so many enemies that made me strong. Let us give thanks for our mothers who gave us a life on the Earth. Let us give thanks for our fathers whose genes gave us a life on this Earth. There are so many things to be thankful for — for the sun we see, for our eyesight, for the sound of music. I give thanks for all of you who have so faithfully come and listened to me. I give thanks for the fun in your hearts that makes you laugh. All of you quietly now give thanks inside yourselves. How many things can you give thanks for? Make a long list.

I give thanks for Mary and her sweetness. May we feel you now, Mary.

I give thanks for the UFOs, the Brothers of Light, who have faith in us that we can make this world work.

In this silence let us each pray that in these elections that are coming up the right people will be elected, that divine guidance will come and elect the correct people to bring us out of the troubles that we are in. Please let the right ones get in office.

This moment I ask for those who are ill that you open yourselves to and allow in the holy power of healing that is flowing in this room right now. Oh, let it flow upon you right now, that you can give thanks, that you can walk out straight.

Those who are depressed, give up your depression. Put the wall of light around, the force field of God around you. Those who came for healings, accept your healing this moment. O healing angels, come and touch them. Skanda, ride over them and touch them. Let the healings take place this moment. Let the Holy Spirit be upon you.

I will pray like I do on the telephone. This is the way I pray on the telephone when someone calls me and they are ill: Jesus. Jesus. Jesus. You have said that if we ask in your name, it shall be done. I'm asking right now, Jesus, for anyone who's ill in this audience here, that you touch them this moment, that they feel your presence. Let it enter them, and let Mary be on the other side. Saint Therese. Saint Martin. Please, Jesus, I ask you again and I ask you again, heal these beloveds right now.

All of you who need a healing, accept the healing. You have to accept it with faith. Believe in a miracle.

Jesus, touch everybody here with your great power. Send your healing angels down right now and touch these people who need a healing of body, mind and soul. Let the power come upon them right now.

We do give thanks. Say, "I thank you for my healing." Go home and believe and go to bed and wake up whole. Say, "I believe in miracles, and I thank you, God, for my healing." Give thanks ahead of time.

Love is flowing here now. Love is flowing. Please let a healing take place. Please believe this moment. This moment is yours. This is your moment now, not tomorrow. Right now is your moment. For this we give thanks.

To everyone, to those who are not here tonight, who are tuning in — one person in India called me today — I send out love on the wings of God. Let us send it around the world.

Put your hands upward and receive. Now put your hands out to the world and give your blessings. Everybody — don't anybody not do it. Now make a dome over the world with your hands and bless it. Bless it. Make a dome over the world — over Washington, D.C. or anywhere else in the United States or in the whole world.

I give thanks. I give thanks. I am grateful. I am grateful. I am grateful.

There is not much more to say except that we all give thanks deep in our hearts for being ourselves. Love yourself this moment. Love yourself. Every morning love yourself. Look in the mirror and love yourself. Be glad you're you. Don't want to be anybody else. Just be you.

Have you ever loved yourself? Not in the form of ego, but just because you have taken a form for God down here to do His work. Love yourself with all your heart. Love. Love is the key.

Anybody who feels they got a healing this night, would you stand up? Thank you. You see, there is no disease that is too big for God. We make it big in our minds because we read the newspapers. Do you understand that? AIDS is not too big for God. Nothing is too big for God. There is no problem in the world that is too big for God. You and God are a majority.

What else is there to say? Nothing. We'll all go home, and in the morning you'll look in that mirror and you'll tell yourself how wonderful you are. If you don't have a job, say, "Oh, I have the most wonderful job in the world. I am so abundant. I have so much money. Oh, it's wonderful." Stop grouching to God, because God gets every one of your messages up there, and He says, "Oh, she has no money. Oh, she doesn't want to have any money. I get the idea. That's what she's talking about, no money, no money." Say, "Oh, God, I have so much it's overflowing, and the abundance is blessing the world." Before you know it, it will be happening.

Trust. Come on, kids, wake up inside. Wake up tonight. Let this be the night when you wake up and you are no longer a caveman. You don't have to have self-preservation because you'll have God-preservation from now on.

Remember, you are the light.

Chapter Nine

My Story

Tonight I'm going to tell you some stories.[1] I've come here to share with you some ways to get over the last little things in us. I can see that you're far advanced, but it's the last little bit, that last little climb up the mountain which is the hard part. The first part is easy because, oh, gee, it's so much fun. Miracles are happening. You call me on the phone and you say, "You know what happened to me? Oh, I got a new car. I prayed and I got it. Somebody gave it to me." We're into what I call pseudo-religion. Sure, we should have some miracles. I just adore them. Wait until I tell you about Sai Baba's miracles — they're wonderful. But they are not the final goal.

Yes, we can give up all and yet not really have given it up in the deep recesses of the caverns within, which we have been afraid to face, because we have a feeling of unworthiness. So, tonight we will take up this deep cleansing.

What I have to give comes from great teachers that I have met on this plane and on other planes which people call heavens, or lokas. I am talking about the Masters of the Great White Lodge. When I started on this path, I was a young, ardent dancer. One day I went to a church and there were only about six people in the church. I was so flabbergasted that nobody was going to church because I had been agnostic and had just started to get into this thing of churches. When I came home, I decided to change my whole dance routine completely and to make it spiritual. I decided to take God to people through my dance if they wouldn't go seeking God out at church. As I said, I was young and ardent and full of pizzazz — I guess you would call it divine pizzazz — because I had read that God spews out of His mouth the lukewarm. Boy, that is something — the lukewarm, the half-way people. I prefer to say I had an obsession, but what an obsession — a divine obsession for God. That is what you here, all of you, also have or you wouldn't be sitting in this meeting, especially on the floor, when you could be sitting comfortably at home.

Let's start with the Masters, or a few I've had the great honor and privilege to know and be with. Would you like to hear about them? It's not who I met that's important, but the fact that in your own lives somewhere, maybe in the Himalayas or some place in the heavens, somebody is watching you and looking over you. Do you understand this, everybody? You are being watched and as you expand, they give you more and more teachings when you go to sleep at nighttime.

The first teacher I met was supposed to be a yogi, but he was a bogey. But what a bogey! He taught me wonderful things. He taught me Vivekananda. He taught me Ramakrishna. He taught me Jesus. And he taught it beautifully. He didn't live it, but then, that wasn't my problem. You see, he put me through the most austere things that anyone could go through.

We were a nice household. On the first Thanksgiving after Dad had passed on, we were sitting at dinner when we found out that Mother was into something. A short time before, our dog had gotten lost. Somebody who was into the Bhagavad Gita brought the dog back and invited Mother to the meetings she was holding. So we were at this Thanksgiving dinner with guests, and my mother stood up and said, "I have to go now," and she walked out. We all looked at each other and said, "Where's Ma going?" You know, in the middle of dinner. But what that lady had said was, "If God is not more to you than a Thanksgiving dinner, then you aren't into it. I want everybody at the meeting on Thanksgiving." So, my mother went. What do we put first? What's our priority? Is it God or the world? Is it God or our family? In Jesus' case, when people said to him, "Your family is at the door," he said, "No, my family is in here." Do you remember that from the Bible?

Then a yogi who was on his way back to India was staying in town. Mother said that there was going to be a class, and I said that I'd come and listen. From then on, it was hell-bent for heaven for me. He said, "Sit down on the floor." I sat, and he pulled one leg over and the other leg over into a lotus position and said, "Don't move until I tell you." Two hours later I thought I was going to die, but I didn't move. I felt I couldn't move, that I mustn't move. I don't know — it was something inside me. I didn't know what this was all about, but I knew it was something.

Then he said to me, "Would you give one hour a day for peace?" I thought that behind this there was something going on, and I was a little scared to say yes because I thought it was going to make a big change in my life. I was a dancer, and I was full of fun, having a nice time on Earth, and life was just great. I thought for a while and I said, "Yes," and the moment I said yes, I knew that I had signed up with the right gang, on God's side. Do you understand what that meant when I said, "Yes, I will give an hour a day for peace"? I've given more than an hour a day for peace since then — I've given twenty-four out of twenty-four.

This yogi put me through things you wouldn't believe. Whatever I did was wrong. If you don't like people criticizing you, you should have had him as a teacher. But, you see, I believed that he was a God-man, and I believed that he was testing me. Because he was testing me, whatever he did or said was okay, and I had to do it. If you only knew, my beloveds, that somebody is watching you and testing you at all times, you wouldn't fall under ego, pride, any of those things. Do you follow this? They are watching.

He would say, "All right, now you be master of ceremonies." Afterwards he would say, "You spoiled the whole show, you spoiled it completely." If a tear ran down my cheek, he'd say, "Don't be a fool." In front of everybody, he'd call on me, and he'd put an extra "a" in my name. My name is Charlton and he'd make it Charlatan, "Hilda Charlatan." There'd be all these eyes looking at me. Then he'd tell me how horrible I was if I reacted in any way. I remember once we were all in the country and I happened to turn my head to look at a flower. He said, "All right, don't move. Meditate. Don't move." For the next two hours, I had to meditate in that position. If you've never meditated with your neck crooked, just try it for fifteen minutes. I couldn't get it back straight again after he said I could move. He put me through these disciplines.

Once he said, "I'm going to test you. You are not to speak a word until I give you permission," and he gave a two-hour lecture. He threw a power at me that all I wanted to do in the whole world was to interrupt him. I wanted to, but I bit my lips, I held my lips. I did everything I could do to keep from talking. All I wanted to do was to interrupt that bogey, but I didn't. At the end he came up and said, "Well done." Because as the energy comes up, if it comes out the mouth, uncontrolled, it can't go up to Mount

Everest, the crown chakra. It has to go all the way up. The energy that's in the lower part goes up the spine and goes up to all your chakras. If it hits the navel, it's power. If you get stuck on power, it's too bad if you haven't got love. That's what many, many teachers who come here from the Orient get stuck on — power. After the third chakra, then the energy goes up to the heart, the fourth chakra, and you have love. When you mix these two, then you've got something. When the energy gets up to the throat, you speak divine words. Then when the energy gets to the third eye, it has to go on all the way to the top of the head.

So, those were the tests he put me through, that first yogi. I was so delighted when I saw him off on the train after three months. I couldn't wait to see the train pull out. Why? Because I wanted to try some of the things he had taught me. I wanted to put them into action.

The next teacher I met was a true master — Yogananda. Would you like to hear a little bit about him? I went to Santa Barbara to see Helen Bridges, who was the artist who drew Babaji, the great master, under Yogananda's guidance. She had a room about the size of this small stage as an ashram for Yogananda, Paramahansa Yogananda. He came in — there couldn't have been more than ten of us there — and when he was talking, I saw a light coming out of his eyes and entering me, just light entering me. At the end he was standing at the door to shake hands and I thought he'd say, "My beloved, you have come." He didn't — he just shook my hand and I went out into the air of Santa Barbara in ecstasy.

Later, because I was overdoing my yoga, I became quite ill. If they said breathe in for seven counts and hold for fourteen, I thought if I breathed in for fifty and held for one hundred, that would be better. I just wanted to make it fast to the goal, but you can't make it fast to the goal. You can't pull a rose open. It has to blossom on its own — you just can't pull it. You have to let yourself unfold.

I was feeling ill and I thought if I could only get to that Yogananda. A friend and I were going into Santa Barbara. I told her not to drive me to where we were going, but to drive me up to Helen Bridges'. When we got there, a car was waiting, and Helen said, "We have a place in the back seat. We're going down to see Swami Yogananda in Encinitas and we're waiting to see who belongs in the empty seat." I said, "Well, I do." All the way down, I was so ill I thought I'd never make it there. They put me in a glorious room with satin curtains overlooking the ocean. I was sitting there thinking that

I was dying when there was a knock at the door. I shall never forget it. I'd never dreamed that the Master would come to my room. I said, "Come in." The door swung open and there was Yogananda, around him a light, an effulgence that filled the doorway. I was instantly healed. He didn't have to say, "Get healed." It was fantastic. Then he asked, "Do you want to learn?" I said, "Yes, I'd like to learn." So he said, "All right, come with me to Mount Washington." So I got in the car and rode with him. Now, I don't know how you people are, but I always thought that holy people should talk holy, they should talk God, you know, heaven. All he talked about on the way was that I should drink carrot juice and eat carrots and raw foods. He was really holistic. I thought, what's up with this yogi? Where's the spirituality? All he's talking about is food, about eating the right things. Yet, every yogi I've ever met has told me the same thing.

So I went to the Mount Washington ashram, which was a great big place. One time I made an appointment to go and see him. I was supposed to have an appointment at seven in the evening. It got to be seven, eight, nine, ten, eleven, twelve, one, two. At three in the morning, they came down for me and I went up to where he was. It was just a heaven up there. He didn't really sleep, you know. He slept maybe one hour a night. We had our interview about 3:00 in the morning. I sang for him. I did some Mayan chants that had been given to me in meditation and he said they were genuine. He said, "Would you stay with me? I will have a place for you at the ashram." I thought about it the rest of the night, and I had to say no to him because I didn't want to, what shall I say, be caught in anything. I didn't want to join anything. I wanted to be a free soul. Do you understand that? To be a free soul, not to be bound by any one thing. It's too limiting. I felt it was too limiting for me. So I went my way, and much later, when I was going to India, he gave me letters of recommendation and we had a lovely talk.

Then I went off to India. Because I didn't have the money to go to India, I went as a dancer, a classical dancer, danced everywhere in India and then I stayed there. I was in Ceylon for a while. I will tell you just a short story of a yogi — Yogi Swamy. He was exactly what you would think a yogi would look like — soft gray hair, grey beard, elderly, wonderful. When I used to go to see him, I would travel all night on an old train to Jaffna, where all the warfare in Ceylon is going on now. This one time I had brought some camphor.[2] The day before, my friend had taken somebody there who wanted to know about a lot of worldly things. When this person went in there, the yogi had asked him, "What have you got behind your back?" The man had said, "Camphor," and the yogi had said, "Burn it on your own tongue." Yogis could be tough, kids. Then he said to my friend, "Why do you bring people of that caliber here?" So I came in the next day. I had some camphor behind my back. I had just heard this story. He asked, "What have you got behind your back?" I said, "Camphor," and he said, "Come right in, come right in." See?

Every time I went there, he would say, "How much money do you have?" It was just like Yogananda with the food — I would think, what kind of a person is this? I would give no answer, and then he would know I had no money. He would ask, "What is your salary?" Well, I didn't have any salary. So one day I was honest with him and I said, "I don't have any money." He said, "Oh." He had a boy take a book and read, and as the boy read, this yogi sat there moving his hand a certain way. The boy read, "There is an upper jaw and a lower jaw and the tongue is the conjunction. The tongue makes the sound and the sound is prosperity," and the yogi said, "What is that word? You mispronounced it. How do you spell prosperity?" The boy spelled it out. All the while the yogi was moving his hand, doing something, you understand? I never had money trouble after that. I want you to know that you have the same opportunities. Do you understand this?

One time before I went to India, I was taking care of my mother's house. I had been living in Santa Barbara and had come back, and I was doing housekeeping for her. She was in the real estate business, and I was taking care of the money, the household money. I was spending this money on household things, and when I got down to three pennies, I took the three pennies. The Masters, the invisible Masters of the Great White Lodge, had come to me by then and were training me. I heard my Master say, "If you steal three pennies, you would steal big money if it were ever put in your hands." I said, "Oh, rot," and I took the three pennies. I went out that day in my old jalopy and — putt...putt...putt — it ran out of gasoline. I walked to a gasoline shed and I said, "Give me one gallon. That's all the money I've got." But inside I said, "No. I have abundance." I went back to the car, poured the gasoline in, looked in my purse, and where there had only been just enough for one gallon, my purse was full, because I had declared that I had the abundance of the universe. I went back to the gasoline shed and without counting, I said, "Give me five gallons." And guess how many cents I had over when I paid for the five gallons? Three cents — and did I hear the Master laugh! I heard him chuckling, "Ho ho ho ho."

I was into pseudo stuff then, you know, what we call demonstrating. I had this jalopy and I would say, "My gasoline tank is always full. My gasoline tank is always full." And sure, it was always full. I was manifesting it. But one day it went bomp, bomp, bomp and stopped. Somebody came over to help me, and I said, "Is there any gasoline in the gasoline tank?" He said, "Yes, it's full, but the gasoline is not running into the engine. The fuel line is blocked." Do you understand the power of that? When we pray, we've got to pray the right way. I only prayed half a prayer. I only prayed to make my gasoline tank full. I didn't say, "Run my car, God." Be careful of your prayers because you'll get them answered, but they had better be a whole prayer of what you want.

Now to talk about some of the other Masters. I would like to talk about Mahadevananda, who was my yoga teacher. He was 160 and he looked about 45. He was wonderful. His body had decayed and he had lost his teeth and had gone to the Himalayas and regrown himself and had come back. When I met him, he was about 160. He belonged to an order that never looked at a woman for the first 90 years. He said he didn't know what he had been missing until the 90 years were up. He was wonderful, just simply a wonderful, wonderful person. I could talk a long time about him. Even now I have a photograph of him, and once in a while, if there is any concern going through me, I can hear the photograph say, "Don't worry, Hilda, don't worry." I hear him speak through it. I could talk a long time on each of these Masters, but we have to get on with the lesson.

Nityananda's is a wonderful story, and this is the story I want you to understand. Nityananda — he was not a man. He was God. He was found under a bush, not born through a woman, and a harijan, a poor woman, picked him up and took him home. She couldn't make him eat anything. She was going to put him in a basket — like Moses' story — and put him on the river near where he was found and let him, this tiny baby a few days old, float away because he couldn't eat. Then a holy man came along and told her to put a bit of crow's meat in the baby's mouth. At the same time that the holy man spoke, a man came along with a crow. The woman just touched the baby's tongue with the crow's meat. Do you understand what that did? It brought his vibratory rate down from the ethereal into this plane of consciousness which we call the physical.

Now if any of you get too ethereal, don't eat crow's meat. Just eat soya burgers, but eat something, just eat something. A person called me one day and he said, "I'm so ethereal, I don't know what to do. I'm bleeding from somewhere." I forget from where, his mouth or something. I said, "Well, go and eat something." He said, "Well, oh, good, I'll eat a lettuce leaf." I said, "Oh." I sent someone out there to teach him how to eat — how to eat lentils and beans, how to eat properly, holistically, a balanced diet. So when you're getting too ethereal, and you're walking up above the Earth and your feet don't touch the Earth, and you're getting nervous, go and have a good meal. Do you understand? I'm giving you practical stuff now because I'm not likely to come to Princeton again. So gather it all in.

My own story with Nityananda is wonderful. I was in my house in Oakland, California, breathing in and out, breathing in and out. Oh, my God, I had read in Vivekananda's book to breathe in so many, hold so many and breathe out so many, and I was doubling it and tripling it, and I was feeling a fire inside me. I was burning myself to pieces with this ardency. Then, boom, in the corner of my room appeared a yogi and he even brought a tree, under which he was sitting. I looked at the yogi. It lasted for maybe forty seconds, maybe a minute, and faded away. Then I could breathe, I could hold, I could do everything. He gave me grace. He looked over from India where he was, in Ganeshpuri, and saw this fool of a girl, blowing herself to pieces, and he said, "Let me help her." So he helped me. There will always be someone to help you. Do you understand that? There will always be someone to help you. I am telling you this. You are never alone. Never alone.

Years later, in India, I was in a taxi cab where I saw a picture of a holy man. In the Orient, the cab drivers will have a picture of their guru in the taxi, and they'll put Christmas lights around it. Now, if someone here took a taxi cab and put Jesus' picture in it and lights around it, I'm sure that cab driver would be called into the office and given his pay. But there, they do that and the lights go blinking on and off. So I was in this taxi cab and saw this picture and I said, "Who is that?" The driver said, "It's a great, great Master, way up in the jungles outside Bombay." I made up my mind that I'd go and see him — and so I did. I went to Shirdi Sai Baba's shrine and there I met a lady who said, "Let's go to Ganeshpuri." When I got there, who was it? Well, there's a story before that that I want to tell you.

I was up in Delhi. There were three of us, a man who had been in an airplane accident, his sister and I. I was just asking myself, "What is this all about? Why don't I go back to the world?" In the hotel I started to walk up and down like a mad woman. I said, "If I don't see my Krishna today, I'll never see him in this life. If I don't see my Krishna today, I'll never see him in this life." I went down the hall of the hotel to my friend's room and I said, "We're going to Brindavan." I didn't know where Brindavan was, but it was Krishna's place. So the man said, "I'm sick, I've had that accident." I said, as I thought at him with concentration, "How do you feel now?" He said, "Well, I feel better now." I said, "Well, let's grab our luggage, let's go." So we got to Brindavan and we got in a tonga, which is a two-wheeled cart. The driver was taking us to the temple. I went crazy again. I said, "This tonga is taking us to the wrong place. Ask that man." The man on the street was kind enough to jump in the tonga with us and take us to the temple of Krishna. When we got there, he said, "I have to leave you now. I'm going to my master." Again I went mad. I said, "Then take us to your master." He was embarrassed. He said, "Well, I don't know that I can," but he did.

So we walked through the streets of Brindavan with him. Oh, kids, in India you walk through the streets at six o'clock and out of every house is coming the smell of incense. Everybody is lighting incense and the streets are full of it, especially in Brindavan, the land of Krishna. When you come to Brindavan you see Krishna everywhere. Everything is Krishna. People drive cabs for Krishna. People dance for Krishna. People live for Krishna.

So the man took us up to the master. I had an awful sciatica pain from being in Delhi in the cold and not having proper clothes, so I was sitting there and leaning back. This master said, "Sit up and don't be lazy." Did I sit up! Then the ida and the pingala went "woooo woooo" up my spine. He did it for me and he kept me on the path.

And so later, I was in Bombay, and we decided to go to Ganeshpuri. As soon as I got there and looked at the Master, Nityananda, I knew he was the one who had helped me in Oakland, California, ten thousand miles away, and in Brindavan. Do you understand this, my loves? There is somebody looking over you. No matter if you feel deserted or as if you have nobody, if you are striving, you are not alone. There was a line of people that went past him, and he would just sit there. He was just God Almighty, that's all. I froze. Perspiration dropped off of me and I couldn't move. I went into samadhi standing there, and the people went around me. When I came down, I ran around, got into the line again and came through again to see this great being because I had found my own at last. I knew I didn't have to look any more. When you find your own, you know it in your heart. Your heart stops looking around. It may be Jesus, it may be yoga, it may be just a truth inside yourself, but when you've found it, you don't have to look any more. It's wonderful.

After that, I would go and see him. I'd ride the old third-class train with the women and the fish mongers and the smell of fish and the yelling of "mahla, mahla, mahla," which means fish. Then I decided to go stay there for a year. I thought that I would go there and just make it to God. And I heard him say, "Write and ask how I am." I wrote to a man who was the head of the Iron Department, who was his disciple, and he said Nityananda had passed on. I went to Ganeshpuri, and I stood in front of his chair and I said, "What did you do this for? I was coming here to stay a year with you. Why did you do this?" I heard him say, "You shall never see me again except as the Atma, or God, in your own heart." He was a tough one, I'm telling you. He was the best teacher possible. We talked mind to mind. We didn't talk with words. We didn't use words. The only thing he would ever say was to grunt "Unh, unh." I met a person much later and I said, "You knew Nityananda? Did he ever say anything wonderful to you?" He said, "Yes." I said, "What did he say?" He said, "Unh."

To bring this story up to date, in New York I went shopping by myself recently, something which I never do. I came out of the store alone with my money purse open, and this guy came toward me to grab my purse. I went at him like this, "Unh." Did he run! I'll tell you, it's better than guns. It's better than mace. It's better than anything. Nityananda did it inside me. Do you understand? Then I turned around and the guy was coming back. He was looking at me. I went "Unh," and that poor guy was scared stiff. He ran. I don't blame him, with that noise. Nityananda took care of me. I was such a fool to stand with my purse open on Broadway and 103rd, which is a bad part of town. You don't do those things where poor people are, because you make karma for others. You make karma for others if you're careless with your purse.

After Nityananda passed on, someone told me about Sathya Sai Baba. I wanted to go to his ashram. I went to buy a round-trip ticket. The station manager at the railway said, "Have you asked the Master?" meaning Sai Baba. I hadn't gotten there yet so I got a little irritable. I said, "Asked the Master? What for? Give me a ticket back in three days. I am going back to America." He said, "I can't give you a return ticket. You didn't get permission from the Master." I stayed about fourteen months straight with Sai Baba.

When I finally got there, it was very late at night, after the lights were all out — the lights go out at 9:30 at his place. I didn't know where to sleep or anything. It wasn't as organized as it is now. It wasn't organized at all. If you wanted to go to the bathroom, you'd walk to the mountain, find your favorite rock, and that was your toilet. I had a favorite rock.

Because I got there very late at night, they put me on the hospital veranda. When I woke up, there was a mangy dog sleeping with me. I woke up about 4:30 a.m. with a power coming at me. It was the same power that I had felt at Nityananda's, at 4:00 in the morning, when he had sent this "wooo" as electricity through me. Not very comfortable electricity, either. I had looked around, and everybody was sleeping. I had said, "What's the big idea, Nityananda? I mean, everybody else is sleeping, why wake me up?" I had tried to go back to sleep, but I couldn't. I had to sit up and meditate. So the same thing happened at Baba's. This "wang" came at me and I said, "Boy, I've hit the jackpot here."

Usually you wait maybe weeks and weeks and maybe years to get an interview with Sai Baba, but I just walked out there that morning and he came out. He motioned to me, but I didn't know what he meant. People said, "He's calling you in for an interview." I said, "What's that?" They said, "Go, go, go," so I went in. He looked at me and he said, "That's yogic heat. She has yogic heat." From overdoing, you understand. Then with a motion of his hand he took some halvah out of the air — it was still hot out of somebody's pan — and he said, "That's heat, this is sweet, eat." I ate it and my whole system cooled off. He did many, many things for me, many, many miracles. People say that if you're a high soul, you won't do miracles. Well, believe me, I enjoyed those miracles, and it didn't do any harm. When he was criticized for doing miracles, Sai Baba said, like a little boy, "Why shouldn't I take from Sai stores? Other people give presents, why shouldn't I take from Sai stores and give to the people presents?" I'll tell you, miracles awaken you into another dimension. When you first see him wave his hand in the air and holy ash or a ring or something else comes in his hand, you burst into a fourth dimension of consciousness. It makes it seem that we are living in such a dull, clucky way down here. We live in three dimensions, and if somebody goes into a fourth dimension, we say he shouldn't do it.

I spent a long time with Sai Baba. He took me around with him, and I never became so dull that I didn't like miracles. You know, after a while, you can say, "Oh, he made holy ash," and then the next day, "Oh, he made holy ash. Oh yeah, he made some holy ash." But never with me. For me it was, "He made some holy ash! Oh, wow! He made a locket — wow!" One time a girl gave him a gold locket with the symbol "om" on it and he said it was a rotten om. Then he said, "Would you like an om or a picture of me?" She said, "I would like a picture of you." With that, he went like this — whooh — and where there had been just a plain little locket, there was a beautiful thing with his picture with twenty-three diamonds around it for the twenty-three years that this girl had been with him and had served him. As he blew, it made me feel what it must have been like when God blew us into creation.

This ring I wear is Sai Baba's. He made it out of the air. I had been going around to temple after temple and gathering holy ash for healing work for when I came home and had been putting it in my trunk. Nobody knew this. The last day I was with Sai Baba, he called me up and he said, "Hilda has a trunk full of holy ash for healing. I'm going to give her a ring." He did this "shoop" and the ring was there. He said, "If you look in it, you will sometimes see me or sometimes it will go into the infinite and it will just turn into light." And it has. There have been hundreds and hundreds who have looked into this ring and have seen him in color, walking. It has been a magical ring.

It isn't the trinkets. No. It is not the holy ash. No. It is what we are coming into in the Golden Age. Do you understand this? This is what we're going to be. It's a forerunner. All I can say is that you are being watched and loved. If you are sitting here, you are known. When a light of aspiration and inspiration comes over your head, the Masters say, "There's one we must teach." They will take you at nighttime and not let you wander around on the astral planes, but will take you and teach you. There is a place where the Masters teach us at nighttime. You know all these things, but you've got to have the desire to go ahead.

I'd like to remind you about one more thing. Look in the mirror in the morning. If you're ill, if you're feeling sick, if you think you're ugly, if you think everything is going wrong for you, look in the mirror in the morning and say, "I am beautiful. I am radiant." If you're forty-two, say, "I am twenty-four." Turn it backwards: "I am twenty-four and wonderful. I am healthy. I am glorious. I am wonderful. I am wonderful. I am wonderful."

Start your day like that, looking in the mirror. So use the mirror positively to reflect your true, wonderful divine Self. The Master said not to look to the outside of people, but to look to their souls. No matter how they're acting outside, look to their souls. And so, look to your soul and see your perfect Self.

Why should we be miserable? Why should we be sick, when we have a mind that can create a new life for us? If you haven't got a job, go to the mirror and say, "Oh, thank you, God, for my wonderful job." If your boss is mean, you say, "Oh, my boss is so wonderful." You'll go down and he'll be wonderful. Change your life. Be the master of your own life. Do you understand me clearly? Hallelujah! That's the extent of my evangelism.

Be not afraid of anything. Come into the heart. Come home and accept yourself just as you are. Will you accept yourself just as you are? There's no one up there who judges you. No angels judge you; no Jesus judges you, no Mary judges you, no Moses judges you, no Elijah judges you. We are the stupid fools that judge ourselves, and we go on judging and judging and judging.

Will you give up your iniquities this moment and say, "I will not judge myself. If they don't judge me, I won't judge myself anymore"? Accept yourself this moment just as you are. With every bit of sin that you've done, everything wrong that you've done, accept it as stepping stones to this moment. It is only a school down here. Does Jesus not say, "Come unto me all ye who are heavily laden"? Those who are heavily laden, place your burdens at his feet tonight, at those sacred feet that were bloodied for us. That Jewish man went upon the cross so that we could be turned toward another direction, a new direction, and a life abundant — abundant in love.

Take the words as I say them — just loving for love's sake, not depending on someone to love, just love flowing for the sake of flowing, working for work's sake, and living lives for the sake of freedom. Oh, beloveds, you are indeed blessed. Let us turn our backs on the ways of Adam. Adam was our father. When Adam fell, what did he fall in? Not into a fig leaf, my kids. He fell into self-consciousness, and we have been self-conscious ever since. If you ask somebody, "Who are you?" he'll say, "I am Bill." He doesn't say, "I am God." We lost God-consciousness with Adam. When Jesus went on the cross, he went as a ram, as a sacrifice on that cross. Before that he had a conference with Elijah and Moses, and they discussed it, the three of them. He said, "I am going to do this to break the Adamic law of self-consciousness and transform self-consciousness into God-consciousness."

That's what we are coming into. No longer are we going to be self-conscious from this night onward. We are to turn our backs on the way of Adam. That was when we as a race became self-conscious, egocentric personalities, I-and-me-conscious. It has all been a big nightmare for thousands of years, a terrible dream. Let us awake and know help is at hand this very night. The climb is steep, but the rewards are great; the air is fresh and rare. Jesus has trod this pathway ahead of us so we cannot go astray or get lost. When he left this Earth, not through death, but by rising above the density of the Earth, he sent the Holy Spirit to comfort us until he returned. This is his dispensation and he shall come again with Moses and Elijah by his side.

I'm going to ask that the Holy Spirit come to us this moment. I would ask you to do one thing. I would have you close your eyes and do some work. I want you to see down below in a valley a muddy stream, and I want you to see yourself up on the mountain looking down on that muddy stream of earth. Ask God this moment whom you should help out of that muddy stream. Look down there and you will see somebody. Put your hand out mentally to the person. Drag the person out of that mud and mire at this moment and it will happen out in the world. You do it intellectually and spiritually here, but it will happen to them out there. Put your hand down to somebody that's in drugs, in drunkenness, or in travail. Let God show you who it is that you have to help tonight. Put your hand down deep. Walk toward that mud, but don't fall in it. Start pulling people out. Pull them out onto the mountain, and keep pulling them up until they are safe. It might be somebody you love and can't help, who won't listen to you talk about God. We'll do it this way.

Ask God again, "Is there anybody else down there I need to pull out?" Put your hand out. Drag them out of the dirt quietly, with love. I'll be silent while you do it. Oh, yes, God, we're on Your side, God. We're going to save as many souls as we can that they won't have to go into the hell of what is coming.

With your eyes closed, just listen to me. Those who would like to make a commitment to their own soul's perfection and ask to be bathed in the light of the Holy Spirit will have a great opportunity in this next minute or two. Think what your obstacles are that the Light can dissolve. I will chant the sounds of God from the ocean of God.

I ask that the Holy Spirit be here. All of you, ask for the Holy Spirit to be here that we can feel it. I would like to feel it, God. I would like to feel it like a cool breeze upon us. I haven't felt it yet. Please, God, let your Holy Spirit descend upon us right now. I will chant to the holy angels and call them.

O Great Infinite Hierarchy, look down upon us and bless us. Bless each one here and look into each one of our souls. Please enter us into the Book of Life. Please let the Holy Spirit come upon us. Let it descend upon us. Believe. Let there be no doubters here. It doesn't cost anything to open our minds and allow the Spirit to work. I will ask the Great Spirit to descend upon us from the heavenly heights as love. May it blow upon us this night into our hearts. May the holy angels cleanse our desires, our bodies and our minds. As the heart directs you, as we sing "Amazing Grace," you may stand as a monument to God. If you don't want to stand, pray for the others who are standing, who have the courage to stand. Those who remain seated, pray for the others. Don't stand until you feel like it. Can you feel coolness on your skin?

Oh, praise the Lord! The Spirit has come.

Oh, amazing grace, that saves souls like us.

Oh, God, I love Thee, I love Thee so much, God, and I love Your children so much.

This moment say: "God, I dedicate my soul. I want my soul to shine in this world. I want to go out and help people. Give me the strength to help people, give me the words to help people, give me the love to help people. Take away all my obstacles inside and let me know that I am forgiven everything I ever did from the time of Adam on. I'm not going to have unworthiness any more. I know they never condemned me up there in the Hierarchy, and I'm not going to condemn myself. It is better to walk with two feet down here on Earth, not condemning myself and helping others on this path."

We will make it, kids. Come what may, we will not be afraid. I hold this candle, for it is you. The light is you. The light is the light within you.

Chapter Ten

Our Goal on Earth

To live, to love, to make it here on Earth should be our aim, our joy. To tread the path set down by those who came to Earth to show the way should be our goal.

We know the way to make our lives glow bright. We know the laws set down by God Himself. These laws, if obeyed, will make a person's life turn right. They were not made to punish, but God knew His creation, man, might falter and put his faith aside, so God made the rules to keep us firm. He said, "Walk tall and right. Love yourself, but love your neighbor too, the same as yourself." He knew what you give out, you get back. In our self-indulgence, our uncontrolled way of being, we learned to hate these laws and even think them unjust. But they are only signs upon the path or, shall I say, walls that line the pathway to keep us going straight, to keep us from going too far astray from the golden light of love.

God gave us a body. What have we done with it? Have we learned the happiness that life can give? God gave us a mind to emulate Him and create through His divine help. Have we created hell or heaven for ourselves with that mind? God gave us feelings that He might love through us on Earth. He sent us down to Earth, down into the Earth-matter to take on a physical body, so that He might love down here through us — because without us He cannot love down here. Do you understand that? We are necessary for the love to come down to this Earth.

And when He sees His sheep are straying too far from the original plan of joy and goodness, love and wisdom, He sends Himself to Earth as prophets, God-men and God-women, to shepherd us back into the green pastures of His love. He sent us Himself in form with so many shapes, so many names, but all the One. God looks down on Earth and says, "This can't go on! I must send someone down there!" What names come before my mind's eye? Elijah, Moses, Krishna, Rama, Baba, and at this season the name of beloved Master Jesus stands out — Jesus, divinity of my heart.

May I share with you this night my heart's love for him as it flows forth? So many years he has been my teacher and my true friend. He first came to me as I learned of yoga one day so long ago, and yet it seems like yesterday, for it is fresh in the memory of my heart. I sat on my bed, crossed my legs in lotus position as in the East, and challenged my new friend who had come into my room. I said, "Jesus, I don't care about your message of two thousand years ago. I don't care about your disciples who lived and walked the Earth so very, very long ago. We're not fishermen or tax collectors. Is your message practical? Does it work for us now? Can your way work right here and now?"

He took my dare, took me by the hand and slowly, gently led me up the path through love to light. Yes, his ways are the most practical of all. "Love thy neighbor as thyself." "Hmm," I said at that time, "Yes, just like yoga teaches. It makes us all one." "He that humbleth himself shall be exalted." Ever try it? I have. It works like a charm. That Jesus, he was a master of the highest form. His ways work right here on Earth and make a path on which we can skip up, dancing, laughing with glee to find how simple it all can be.

Oh, it's so simple, my beloveds. All you have to do is to give up all your little self, all your little isms, all your little ways, all your likes and dislikes, and your intellect. It's so simple! Oh! You just get empty like Krishna's flute. Krishna could blow through the flute because it was empty, and God can only blow through us when we are empty — when we have rid ourselves of all our stupidity that we have collected along the way. It makes us skip up the path, dancing, laughing with glee to find out how simple it all can be. You don't have to do anything. You don't have to go to India. You don't have to go to Greece. You don't have to go to Jerusalem. You don't have to go anywhere. You just stay in your own place and be simple and love thy neighbor as thyself.

The ways of Jesus free us from the burdens we have made because we strayed. He is like the divine alchemist who turns the base metal of our existence into gold.

Let us put out our hand this moment and let him lead us back to the Sea of Galilee — down memory lane, for some of you might have been there, who knows? Let us go back in fancy and see how clear a picture we can form. Let us feel the dust under our feet as we walk in Galilee and see this man in white coming down toward us, mixing in the crowd, not arrogant, not proud, just walking among us with his golden hair and blue eyes. Close your eyes. Be there now. Feel it.

Oh, Jesus, lead us home, my beloved. Lead us home. You came with bare feet and just a robe to tell us to be simple and to go home into our hearts. O Jesus, Jesus, beloved of my heart, forgive my long way in coming back to thee. I walked such a roundabout way.

Let us feel as if we are there now. The disciples are sitting around him, all Jewish people, for there were no others. I see him sitting in the middle. We will stand on the edge unseen and listen to what he has to say. What are you saying to your disciples, my Jesus? Listen inside your head and heart and hear him talk. I hear him say, "If thou hast not loved thy neighbor, then my time on Earth has been in vain. If thou cannot smile and be of good cheer in the midst of the trials down here, then it has been in vain that I took form and came down." And I answer you, Jesus. Forgive us for our foolish ways, as we are but children. We knew not the way. Of course we strayed, but lead us back through love this very day.

And young Mary, the light entering her. Is that too far removed from Ramakrishna's mother, who saw a light enter her womb when her husband was away, and she too knew that she was with child, just as Mary did? This Mary, what faith in God she must have had! Joseph also knew and believed Christ would be born to them. Oh, their problems were so great, for they were not yet wed. The problems of that day were great: all Jews were persecuted, unrighteous taxes were collected. So Mary, burdened with child, had to travel to Bethlehem to register, and Joseph took her there and did the best he could to give her a place to rest. The sky must have been clear, the air cold, when Jesus, son of Mary, came to this Earth, and the shepherds found him there.

How similar the stories of the birth of Krishna and beloved Master Jesus! Krishna, born with the ruler-king fearful lest he take his place in fame, had to be whisked away into hiding in Brindavan lest he be killed. Jesus, lest he be killed by the jealous ruler, was also whisked away to dwell in Egypt. In the cases of both Krishna and Jesus, all male babies born at that time were condemned to die, and die they did at the command of the ruling king. But Krishna and Jesus both were saved and grew to tell their message to mankind.

I heard a Hindu man once say when he had a vision of Jesus, "What a man! What a man!" I said, "Who, who?" He said "Jesus, what a man!" I followed this friend home to see what he would do, and when I entered his house, there he, a Hindu, was decorating it with stars, decorating it for Christmas, for the baby Jesus. Yes, what a man was Jesus, whose message spread thoughout the world from that little village where he was born, not even in a comfortable bed. On Christmas morn, millions of Christians will be worshiping the Christ, born immaculate through a young Jewish girl. How beautiful, how universal, how glorious are the great ones of heaven who plan it all for us down here.

If in your hearts you feel that, in the name of Christ, persecution has taken place upon this Earth, must you then throw out Jesus because his followers don't live his advice and love their neighbors as they love themselves? Have any disciples lived as their Masters have told them to? If we throw out Jesus because much wrong has been done in his sacred name, then we must throw out Mohammed, Buddha, Elijah, Moses — and where will we be then? For have any of their followers lived as they taught? If Jesus on the cross could say, "Forgive them, they know not what they do," then cannot we do the same and accept his glory, his love and his sacrifice, and on this day so close to his birthday, give him honor?

He is my love. He taught me well to love, to live, to forgive others and myself as well, and through his message I learned to laugh at life and dance up the path into the light. All I can say is that we are happy, Jesus, we are glad you paused for a while down here.

For a moment just listen to the air, just listen to it. Let us all listen inside ourselves for a moment. Jesus' presence and the presence of the Masters is here right now. Go into your heart, and for his sake take a nail out by giving up a prejudice, giving up some hate you have. Take a nail out of his hand, out of his feet. Give up your old ways this moment that he may look down and say, "I did not live in vain."

Oh Jesus, save our world for us. Please, Jesus, Elijah, Moses, Masters, believe in us and do not lose faith in us. We can do it down here, we can — I know, I know. What more can we say when it has all been said? The history of his life we know, but have we taken his teachings to heart? These are the things that Jesus taught us two thousand years ago for that which was to come, this travail, this tribulation: he taught us to forgive, to love under all conditions, to keep firm and clear no matter what goes on around us, to react not to the masses that are uncontrollable, and with patience and fearlessness to tread the path of his aim for all the world. His aim is peace on Earth, good will unto those of good will. We must hold with steadfastness to that which he came to accomplish. He has explained it well to teach his close ones to live rightly, fully, and warn others of what might come if the message is not lived.

As I write, I wonder under what guise of the Jesus message comes persecution, or the Crusaders, or Joan of Arc's incarceration, or the Holocaust. We could go on to the present times when those calling themselves Christians are creating bombs to kill.

Let this little group here start to heal his wounds and live in truth and the way of God. Let us rededicate ourselves to truth and start this very night to live the life regenerate. I promise you that when you get the hang of it and it becomes a part of you to be controlled and loving above the Earth's pull and the lower vibrations that try to pull you down, your life will be glorious and full of power.

We are entering a new life — listen carefully — a new way of thinking, a new way of acting, a complete turnabout. We are walking on virgin soil which has never before been trod on this Earth. We are pioneers of the soul, leading humanity back to God.

I go to light the candles now. As we light the candles, make a wish for peace on Earth. Make a wish for the world.

Chaper Eleven

The Last Lesson

On the evening of January 27, 1988, the night before her first scheduled class of the year, Hilda entered the hospital with chest pains. The next night the following lesson that she had prepared was read by a student.

Let us go back into the Garden of Eden, before Adam made his mistake and listened to someone outside instead of to his true Self inside. Before his fall, he had stood naked before God. What does that mean?

The deep understanding of that means that nothing of self was there. He and his Creator were one. Only One did he know. The One in all that he perceived was the One God whom he loved. Whatever he looked at in the panorama before him, he knew as God's Light. So he lived in delight. He lived for his Father, the Great Creator of all. What other reason had he to come down here at all? He came from another planet[1] to bring light to this world, right down here. In shining the light and loving the world, all was clear that his destiny was just to be, not to toil through the day far into the night to make a living to sustain his life. No! He gleaned from God's garden all his needs, fulfilled by God's gracious abundance. Before he even called, the need was fulfilled.

What a glorious plan, what a wonderful way God our Creator planned for all of life! God was our Provider, our Sustainer, our Breath which had been breathed into our nostrils, the very light of our flesh. This great plan of our Father was filled with love, and it was for all of us a gift from above.

He did not plan hardships, trials, despair, disease or travail. God's Infinite Mind cannot think lack or disease. God's Mind only knows the wonder of life, love and will used to please us.

So knowing our heritage, just how did we fall? How did we fall into this deception with this trap of our mind that now believes all is lost, that karma exists, that this world of God down here is so bad? Where, when did this delusion take place?

It took place when Adam began to believe that he too could do all the things his Father could do. He mistook the power he felt surge through him, the love that he experienced, the bliss supreme, as his own. Then came the split. Adam saw himself as separate from the Force of All Things. He became self-conscious, not conscious in God. He thought God was something far, far up above. Slowly this self-ness hardened into hate, greed, avarice and lust. So we have paid the price ever since, thinking that God is not part of us, in us, but is way up above. Now is our time to come back into truth and know that Adam was wrong.

Jesus taught us the truth. Why did that great man give instructions about love, naming his Father in all his talks? Because he wanted to connect us once more to our Source.

First, we just separated ourselves from our Father. Then came the split between brothers and sisters, the forgetting that we are one family with one Father, our God. Then came more separation. We divided the Earth into countries, into sections, and said, "Stay off my turf." As if that were not enough, we divided our great Creator into different names and called them religions and said, "Mine is the best. Yours is far less." How can one God be divided, I ask? He is One, and no man, no woman can break Him apart.

Knowing all this, what shall we do now? Shall we lay down and die, live in despair? No, no, let us rectify the wrong, turn back time. Make a decision this night — whose side are you on?

Right now, know whose love you feel. If you dance, He is dancing through you in glee. If you sing, it is His sounds coming forth right on key. If you write, then whose thought comes forth? If you daily go forth to work, then know that it is He in your footsteps, in your mind. If any clever thoughts come tumbling through, then, oh glory, it is He! It is our Father breaking through the density caused by our ignorance, which started so long, long ago. Can't you see?

How exciting, how exhilarating to know He gives a second chance to go back to that Garden of Eden. In a split second, it can be.

Make the decision right now. Decide you have traveled Earth's way too long, too much. He beckons us back. He awaits His lost children. What parents would not want their children's return? Let us not tarry with a mind filled with doubt. Have we not suffered enough in this delusion of untruth? God awaits our return with arms outstretched, ready to forgive our wayward ways, all those times when we fell from His grace. All we have to do this moment is step over the line of doubt, delusion and ignorance of who we are, and the way will be made clear, the path illumined with light.

There is no more time. The dark clouds are gathering on the horizon. God is giving you this one more chance. I beg you, come forth out of the downward ways. Change your ideas, your desires, your likes into His, and the miracle of alchemy will take place.

Remember! Remember! Think — deep down inside is a little bit of Eden that never was lost. You call it soul. I call it God's Light, God's Truth, God's Life.

Bring it forth this moment, I plead, I beseech, before it's too late, before the Book of Life is closed and locked for this era. Make your decision right now. Say: "God, I've had enough of separation. It is You, my beloved Father, for whom I have longed, whom I have sought in the world. I'll put my life right. I'll love my neighbor as myself and bring God's unity back once more. I'll be kind to my parents and thank them no matter what, for they are but symbols of You, the true Mother/Father-God above. I'll love my sisters and brothers, all parts of the whole. I'll even love my enemies, for don't they need my love even more? I'll forgive and forget all mistakes, starting with myself. After learning to forgive all I've done, I'll forgive all those who have trespassed against me."

I repeat once again, time is short. Make up your mind. Brush the dust of Earth off your feet and march on with those called the saints, who in truth are only us walking straight. Know your iniquities, then let them go, and march forward, head high, chest out, feet firm on terrestrial ground.

Are you not sons and daughters of God? Remember! Remember! Bring forth from deep within memories of who you are, my beloveds. You are princesses and princes, children of the Great King, the Father of Eternal Life. Know yourself right now. Accept your heritage. Go back to the time before Adam came down and re-remember who you are. You know. You know. So take off all your disguises, your facades, and stand once more naked before God.

Chapter Twelve

Hilda Remembered

Hilda passed on at ten o'clock on the morning of January 29, 1988. A memorial service was arranged for Sunday, February 14, Valentine's Day, at the Cathedral Church of St. John the Divine in the large hall of the Synod House, with its beautiful arched ceiling, where she had held her classes for so many years.

More than 2,000 people came to show their love and gratitude — some who had steadily attended her classes for as many as twenty-three years, some who had come only once but had been so transformed as to never forget her.

A program of music and speakers included her hosts at the two places where she regularly held meetings — the Cathedral and the Hindu Temple in Flushing, Queens — two of her students whose work was in the public eye, and the members of her household.

A peach-colored urn containing her ashes was set in the front of the room before the stage so that those speaking faced it and the audience sat around and behind it. At each of her meetings people had brought her flowers, which were placed in vases on a table by her side on the stage. Many, many people brought her flowers on this day, which were arranged around the urn.

As at Hilda's classes, songs of devotion were softly sung by the musicians and the audience before the program began, and soloists sang songs evoking the atmosphere of Hilda's love and teachings. And also as at Hilda's classes, tears and laughter, devotion and celebration of the deepest kind prevailed.

Ingrid: On behalf of everybody I welcome everybody. It's so great for us all to be together in memory of our beloved Hilda Charlton. Some of us here now only came to one meeting. Others only heard a tape of her or heard of her from a friend. Others of us came to almost every meeting for many years. But one thing we all had in common is the experience of being transformed by the presence of Hilda and her Lessons of Life. We have come today to honor her. Her wish was that this be a joyous occasion, because she despised the somber worldly custom of mourning the passing of a soul to the other side. Therefore we will have an afternoon of music, recollections of her life, and the wonderful Mary dance, which will be performed by Kathy. Hilda choreographed this dance and once upon a time danced it herself with incredible grace. Music, poetry, all arts and artists were so very dear to her heart.

To begin, we'll have Dr. Wally, whom we all know.

Dr. Wally: Hello and peace, my brothers and my sisters. Today is February the 14th, Valentine's Day. And it reminds me of "Oh, how I love you, Hilda." I remember the first class I came to. I was brought here by Larry and Ilene and I sat right in front, about eleven years ago. Hilda's words touched my heart and all I could think of was "Oh, how I love you, Hilda." The energies then were very similar to today. I didn't understand them, but I cried and I laughed, and they both were all going on at the same time. Again I felt "Oh, how I love you, Hilda." Someone gave me her phone number a few weeks later and I called her, not knowing what I was going to say. I was surprised that she answered the phone. Again, I spontaneously said, "Oh, how I love you, Hilda" because I didn't know what else to say. She asked me why I called. I said things were happening in my life and I was frightened and very confused. She said, "Please come to the class tonight." It was Friday night. I went to the class and she surrounded me with light, and she had the people pray for me. All fear left. There was no more fear. Not even today. And she brought out in me the goodness, the responsibility, the concern, the integrity, the love, the humanity, all the attributes that she possesses.

Just recently, she wrote a note to my wife, Phoebe. I'd like to read a portion of it, which will remind you of Hilda. She wrote, "To Dr. Wally's patient, kind, serene, noble and loving wife, Phoebe: Here is a little tiny love offering towards your home phone bill that he has run up because of me. I give you full permission to rebuke him once a month, even yell, if you want. The rest of the time, be a patient, kind, serene, noble and loving human being."

Hilda is a patient, kind, serene, noble, and loving human being. She is a dedicated, fully integrated, humane, loving, joyful, peaceful and, oh yes, playful person whose integrity never allowed her to compromise her ideals and who honored and blessed us by her presence.

Today is Valentine's Day, and oh how I love you, Hilda, but I loved you before and I'll continue loving you forevermore. And any time I do a patient, kind, serene, noble, loving act for people or for the planet, I will dedicate it to you.

Ingrid: Thank you, Dr. Wally. With great gratitude, I call upon a very important figure in Hilda's spiritual mission in New York, Dean Morton, the Very Reverend Dean Morton, who is responsible for hosting Hilda's Lessons of Life class here at the Cathedral of St. John the Divine for the past twelve years. I had wanted to say more in praise of him, but he wouldn't let me. Dean Morton...

Dean Morton: I'm full of all sorts of thoughts. First of all, whenever I'm introduced as the Very Reverend, that stops me, because I mean, what does it mean? We had an archbishop here this morning and archbishops are called the Most Reverend. And so I said to the archbishop, "You know, it's okay if someone says, 'You're really the most,' but it's not so great if someone says, 'You're really very,' which is what I am. Hilda would just roar with all of those stupid kinds of things — the Very Reverend, the Most, all of that.

It's so beautiful to see all of Hilda's friends, because I see Hilda when I see you.

I would like to say a couple of things about how Hilda came to the Cathedral. A very old friend of mine is the rector of St. Luke's Church in the Village, where Hilda's public meetings began. But of course they outgrew the gymnasium, where they were held. And so Ledlie called me and he said, "The Cathedral is bigger than St. Luke's and we have this very strange woman here by the name of Hilda Charlton and she has this fabulous meditation group." I said, "Well, tell me a little bit about it." He said, "Well, it's very difficult to describe." I said, "Is she wacky? What do you mean?" There was a pause, and he said, "She's holy." And I said, "Oh! Well, I'll come down." So I came down and went to what was one of the last sessions down there. You should have seen it. How many of you were down in St. Luke's? It was like sardines. I mean, it was absolutely jam-packed.

So I met her, and she said, "I understand we can come up to the Cathedral possibly?" And I said, "Yes." It was simpler to say, "Yes" than anything else. And so she's been here ever since.

And the incidents, oh there are lots of incidents I can recall, but one incident I want to share with you, because I'll never forget it. She had been here about a year, so she had gotten a feel of the Cathedral and we had gotten to know each other. She said, "I want to walk around with you in the Cathedral." I said, "Okay." And so we walked around. This must have been around 1976, because I was going through a lot of trouble. That can happen to anybody. But I was going through a lot of trouble with respect to certain things here at the Cathedral. Not everything that I was doing, such as having Hilda's meditation group here, met with universal approval. And there were even some who would have liked to see me elsewhere. I was really under a lot of heat at that time. And so, as all of us do in times like that, I looked for all the help I could get. Hilda said, "I just want to walk around with you." We were walking around in the Cathedral, and she said, "Do you know the Dean who was here before you?" And I said, "Well, there are a lot of them." She said, "The one who'd gotten into all of that trouble." And I said, "Well, many of them did." And she said, "What's his name?" I said, "Do you mean Dean Pike?" She said, "Yes." She said, "I've been talking to him." Of course, he had died 15 years ago. And I said, "Say more." And she said, "He said you'll be okay." I don't think she knew the politics of the church, but she said, "You're having some trouble. There are people who are really giving you a hard time." I said, "Yes, that's true." She said, "Well, Dean Pike, he knows, he understands, because he went through it too. He just wanted you to know to stick with it and you'll be okay." Then she told me she'd been talking to various of the bishops who were buried around the Cathedral. I said, "What did they have to say?" She said, "Just keep going the way you're going and it'll be okay."

So, I can't tell you what it means at one level that Hilda won't be calling up on the telephone. I'll miss her very much. But at a deeper level, I don't miss her at all, because she's very much here, just like Pike and all those dead bishops. She makes them come alive. That is, I think, the bottom line of what spirituality is for all of us. We move to different places, to different spaces. The continuity is there, because that's why we're here. Hilda was one of those great — not just teachers, but bringers about of the continuity of the experience of the reality, so that you enter into communion with God right then and there. And if that would stop with her death, then the whole thing's a joke. Right? So, there is really no problem, except we'll miss seeing her, you know, on Thursday. But we'll see her shortly. Thanks!

Ingrid: Thank you so much, Dean Morton. It is with great love and respect that I introduce Dr. Alagappan, the chairman and founder of the Hindu Temple Society of North America. He is responsible for founding the Jyoti movement with Hilda's support and inspiration, which honors the Eternal Godhead or the Goddess of Light and which has erected temples to her. He was instrumental in arranging the use of the Hindu Temple in Queens for the Skanda/Jyoti Puja at the full moon of each month, where Hilda delivered the messages of Lord Skanda. Dr. Alagappan...

Dr. Alagappan: Friends, I'm just now coming from a joint meeting of the Board of Trustees and the Executive Committee of the Hindu Temple Society of North America. They passed a resolution, which they've asked me to transmit to this group here. "The Board of Trustees and the Executive Committee place on record with their deep sense of appreciation the sterling contribution made by Ms. Hilda Charlton as a member of the Board of Trustees since its inception on January 26, 1970. Ms. Charlton, besides imparting an ecumenical leadership, has played a major role in developing the Jyoti philosophy and the Jyoti movement." This is the text of the resolution. It speaks for itself.

You see, when the Hindu philosophy came to this continent in the last century, with the aid of Swami Vivekananda, the temples had not come. This Jyoti movement started only in this century and coincided with the Bicentennial celebrations of this great country. But when the effort started to build the temples, one of the first to be built was the temple in Flushing, and somehow God brought Hilda into the group two days before its first meeting. It was started with a fifty-one dollar check. But then, Hilda was there, and so was her grace. Her contribution was, as the resolution states, an ecumenical leadership. You know, all religions are the same. They lead to the same Godhead. So a religion becomes the practice of a set of people in a particular geographic region. Hilda tried to bring this about and dilute the orthodoxy, the rituals, et cetera, of the people who had brought it. Now, the symbol of this temple became a light surrounded by the insignias of all religions: Christianity, Judaism, Buddhism, Islam and so on. So, it is this type of contribution that Hilda made in the beginning. And the temple at Flushing, Queens was a pioneer, in a sense, and it has brought a movement of temples on this continent. There are now over thirty temples and all of them have this ecumenical character. It is indeed an important contribution made by Hilda. Then, as it was mentioned, Hilda has been there right from the start of this Jyoti movement. Shrines have been erected for Jyoti in New York, Houston and Los Angeles. From here, it has gone to India and a major project is now in the making. And it was our hope that we could have invited Hilda to come and consecrate that shrine and the philosophy there.

Let me explain what this Jyoti is. She is the Eternal Godhead which is the Goddess of Light. According to the Hindu legends, the Universal Mother gave the vel[1] of knowledge to a young son of seven, Skanda, to go and do battle. This vel is said to be one of the forms of the Goddess of Light. Given by Shakti, the Mother, this vel of knowledge is also called *Saravanab-havayai* , or sister of Skanda, or jnana or the absolute truth. Now, we go one step from there to say, "What is this jnana, this knowledge?" The knowledge is to see God in everything in all creation. And so social service is the best form of religion. This is the Jyoti philosophy to which Hilda subscribed.

Hilda was at all times in contact with the celestial beings. She was able to transmit the message of jnana. She gave it a vibrant quality by doing these pujas at the Hindu Temple close to every full moon for quite a few years. The interesting thing is, whenever Hilda came to the temple each month that was the time when the temple acquired a new quality of vibration, a sanctity and a presence of divinity far greater than on any other occasion. So, she was always welcome and so was the group.

Now, as a person, I mean, she obviously, as all of us know, was an instrument of God from the word go. She transmitted the orders and the messages of Lord Skanda. She did not believe in acquiring luggage in a journey through life. She couldn't be bothered with worldly goods. She did not cast her eyes on them at all. She didn't want to have disciples — excuse me, her disciples — or institutions or an ashram. She didn't want any of these things. She couldn't be bothered. She could perform miracles. She did quite often. She could cure sick people. She could do things, but she did it in such a low key that she was not even conscious of it. She believed that the technology of religion was not important. For her, the ethics were much more important. Ethics towered above all that. I have a story of an Indian gentleman who learned how to walk on water. He spent ten years doing this. Then he went to a greater sage and said, "Oh sage, I have learned to do something wonderful." He asked, "What?" He said, "I can walk on water." The sage asked, "How much time did you spend on this?" He said, "I have spent ten years learning this." So the sage said, "You idiot! If you only pay five cents, you can go by boat. Why did you waste your time?" You understand? So, there is no reason, no need to acquire all these paraphernalia or capacities. It is better to be good. And that is what Hilda taught us always. Of course, I know, in the Christian world, they always say that so-and-so, after passing away, gets well-deserved rest. I believe that we should not give Hilda any rest. I believe we must make her work for us, keep her in the lotus of our heart, put in our specific prayers and request her to guide us. I believe that we can integrate her principles in our life. That is the best tribute we can pay to her. And if we become, even to a fraction of a degree, a better instrument of God, that's what Hilda would have liked. Thank you.

Ingrid: Thank you, Dr. Alagappan. I'm sure everyone here could speak on the specialness of Hilda and how she so powerfully affected them. However, such a venture would take weeks, even months, so we've asked a few of her students to speak tonight. It is much to our regret that all cannot publicly share their personal account of the miracle of Hilda's life on Earth.

Al: I'd just like to start off by saying that it's really wonderful to see you all here, those of the recent classes and those of long ago and in between. It really makes me very, very happy. We're Hilda's family. We're her children. You're my brothers and sisters. And together we inherit on this Earth what she has given.

Every now and then, since time began, God sends to Earth one of His very own to save an ailing humanity. Our Father sends us a big brother or a big sister to help us younger siblings, stumbling in the dark, to find our way back home. Filled with His love, overflowing with His peace and exuding His bliss, Hilda, Shanti Devi, Lazumma was one with His eternal essence and now is the golden essence of God. This treasure Hilda shared with us, week after week, month after month, year after year. Surely there was no sparseness of God's teachings through our Hilda. As Hilda, we loved her dearly. She made us laugh. She made us cry. She made us feel what it is to be fully human. Most importantly, she made us feel what it is to be fully divine. She made us reach within and touch our own spirit, God residing in our hearts. Her joy was our joy, our sorrow, her sorrow, and when she cried for us, we cried with her. As Shanti Devi, the yogini, and as the Divine Mother, she beseeched us to give and forgive — to give to each other the jewels of God that she has given to us.

Hilda's life was her teaching — a life of giving and forgiving, loving everyone under all circumstances, and remembering, nay, being God. Her words of truth and love ring in our hearts. Our souls reverberated with her every breath. Thousands who attended her classes, and tens of thousands more who knew her, grew closer to God within the shower of her love and grace. She had a divine knack for relating differently to each and every one of us and yet so perfectly meeting the deepest needs of heart and soul. In her presence, we truly felt loved — loved by Hilda and loved by God. Hilda saw God within us and brought Him forth from within our hearts. The Earth was a better place for her presence and a bit lost without her, but through us all she will live on. For as we live her teachings, singing the song of love in our lives, of giving and forgiving, remembering who we are — embodiments of the Divine — Hilda Lazumma, we will march on to the glory of God.

I'd like, now, to read a poem she wrote in her earlier days.

> I behold within God's hand
> My pure and reborn soul,
> Cleansed by His grace am I,
> Like freshly fallen snow.
> This breath is sweet and comforts me
> In moments of my birth,
> For every step I take will be
> His own upon the Earth.
> I will wander through the heavens
> And soar in every sky,
> Melting in Your sea of love,
> You, my God, and I.
> And as I see this world anew
> My heart is filled with bliss.
> There is no greater treasure, Lord,
> For me to find than this.
> Lay down my soul within Your hand
> My soul as free as wind and sea
> The purest flower has grown.

Hilda Lazumma, Goddess of Light, Mother of Liberty, you live forever in our hearts.

Lois: When I first came to Hilda's several years ago, I came and I looked at the class as I'm looking at it now. And I said, in my own selfish way, "There are hundreds and hundreds of people here. How is she going to notice me? How is she going to love me and care about me with all these people?" But when I started to go to her house, I saw how much she loved me, just in all the little ways she cared about me and about all of you, the way she so tenderly and conscientiously read your letters and talked to you on the phone. I came to the understanding that even if she loved ten thousand people, she wouldn't love me any less. She showed me worlds and times and places that I wouldn't know otherwise. She showed me myself.

She was excited about so many things. Each new thing that came along, she was just as excited about that as about the last thing, whether it was vitamins that we all had to take or some new shampoo for balding that all the men were supposed to use. I remember one thing that was a lot of fun, and that I learned a great lesson from: She was watching late night television and Uri Geller came on and he was bending spoons. She got really excited about that and said, "He's bending spoons with psychic power, but we can bend spoons with love. We're going to use the power of love." So there were about twelve of us all sitting around bending spoons in the living room, focusing and just loving the spoons and getting them to bend. There's not one normal spoon in the house to this day. That was what she represented, love and the power of love. She believed that we could do anything with love, and she tried to instill that in all of us.

Someone came to the house and we were sitting in the kitchen reminiscing about Hilda. They said, "You know, when Hilda was alive, I felt like I was under a small microscope, but now that she's not with us in her physical body any longer, I feel like I'm under a giant microscope." She was always aware of everything that was happening and everything around. We always tried to fool ourselves thinking, "Well, maybe Hilda doesn't know about it." But we can't fool ourselves anymore.

That feeling was really present with me the morning they called from the hospital and said, "Come, she might not live through the day." I was in the bathroom getting ready. I was just doing my normal thing and I felt her presence, her spirit come into the bathroom with me, into such a little homely place. She was there. It was so clear that I could hear her talking to me, and I knew that when I went to the hospital, there was going to be no sadness there for me. I just felt an incredible happiness in my soul for her, that she would be where she needed to be to do the work that she needed to do. I knew that she would be there even more for me now than she ever was before and that for each of us, she could be with us in a much more personal way than she could be in her physical presence, because she couldn't be with us all the time then. She can be with us all the time now. I know that she is still on Earth, in our minds and in our hearts.

Danny: When I first went to Hilda's meeting at St. Luke's in I think it was 1972, I was so in awe of how spiritual everybody at the meeting was. I was sure that they would throw me out the minute that they perceived my clunky vibrations and my earthly thoughts. I feel that way at this moment, trying to find the words to live up to Hilda. But then I hear her saying, "Unworthiness! Fooey! Speak like a Master!" Well, I'll give it a try. I always felt that she treated me like a retarded child that she had a great deal of affection for and so she kind of let me get away with stuff that other people didn't get away with. Maybe it's because I lived out of town, I don't know. I'd like to talk about what I've been going through. I don't know about you, but I haven't taken this particularly easily. I know that's not the most cosmic reaction, but it's been a really complicated and not always easy couple of weeks. I was in Los Angeles and the only person who lives in that area who knows Hilda is someone I haven't spoken to in five years. How do you explain to people who don't know her who Hilda was? Someone called me about possibly helping to get her obituary in the *New York Times*. I don't know whether it ever ran, but what would it say? "Hilda, Also Known As The Goddess of Light, Departs. Fifteen Gods Leave With Her."

At this moment, I know that she's here, and I know that many of the Gods who stayed with her are here. Although I could never see you, oh Gods, I'd like to acknowledge you on behalf of all of us and thank you, because her life brought your blessings to us. So many people we learned about through her — Pericles, Suka, Mahadevananda, the Space Brothers, the Masters of the Great White Lodge, the American Indians, Manu, Skanda, Jesus, Saint Therese, Moses, Sai Baba, Nityananda, Yogananda, Sanat Kumara, Ammal, fifty others that I don't recall now, and yet, of course, we came here for her.

My first reaction to Hilda's passing was one of numbness. I tried to bury myself in my work, and every once in a while, when I was driving, tears would come. So I would try to think of why I was crying. As Dean Morton said, "Obviously, she's fine." So I was certainly not crying for her. Unless every word she ever spoke was a lie, she's in a wonderful place most of the time, and right here right now. Then I felt guilty: "God, I should have spent more time with her. Look at the opportunities I missed. I could have gone to the last meeting. I could have called her more." And then I heard Hilda saying, "Guilt is useless, kid." Then I really realized that a lot of what I was feeling, as Lois was saying, was selfish. "What will I do now? How exactly am I going to carry on when I can't call her up and know that just by talking to her, everything I'm doing is somehow realigned and blessed?"

I can only tell you that over a course of time I've come to feel that she's still here. One of the ways I know is, when she was in her body, I would always censor myself. If I thought of doing something, I would say, "Well, what if Hilda finds out?" I notice I still do that, and believe me, it's not because I'm worried about Al finding out. So I know that she's here in this room, and I know she's here in my heart and in my meditations and for all of us.

The other day I was trying to talk to someone about her and I suddenly remembered that she had told us that in times of trouble we could look to the Psalms. I remembered that the psalm that she read so often was the 91st Psalm and I would like to read some of it.

He that dwelleth in the secret place of the Most High
Shall abide under the shadow of the Almighty.

And then Hilda would say, "The secret place of the Most High, kids! Where is it?" And we always knew that we could get there with love. The psalm goes on...

I will say of the Lord, He is my refuge and my fortress.
My God, in Him will I trust. Surely He shall deliver thee
from the snare of the fowler and from the destructive
pestilence. He shall cover thee with His feathers and
under His wings shall thou find shelter. His truth shall
be thy shield and buckler.

And Hilda would say, "That's a promise from God, kids. It's not just a bunch of words on a piece of paper written a couple of thousand years ago. That's a promise from God. Take it into your hearts!"

Thou shalt not be afraid of the terror by night,
nor of the arrow that flyeth by day, nor the pestilence
that walketh in darkness, nor the destruction that
wasteth at noonday. A thousand shall fall at thy side
and ten thousand at thy right hand, but it shall not come

nigh thee.

How many times she repeated that!

She made this group a family. I don't suppose most of us would have known each other if it were not for her. And yet, any time for the rest of our lives, if we see each other on the street, we will remember her love. I call on God this moment to bless every one of us that we stay in harmony, live up to her aspirations for us, spread the light and love humanity and each other as she loved each of us. Thank you.

Karen: So many people have asked what it was like to spend a day with Hilda. Although I'm not sure one could ever say any day was a typical day with Hilda, I think the best you could say is that each day was an adventure and that no two days were ever alike. But one day does come to my mind and I would like to share it with you.

Hilda got me up one morning and she said, "Karen, are you hungry?" I said, "Yes." She said, "Well, we can eat later." She said, "How would you like to go to Broadway? I'd like to get a gift for my goddaughter. I thought we could go to some of the stores." Now Hilda had some favorite stores on Broadway. Her favorite one was Weber's. There were a lot of discount stores on Broadway, and she had great fun looking in them and trying to get a good buy.

So we got dressed and on our way to Weber's, at 104th and Broadway, there was a lady who was lying on a bench. Her legs were very, very swollen. She was a bag lady. Hilda stopped and she looked at her and she started to talk to her. She looked at me and there were tears in her eyes. She said, "We've got to do something for her. She's cold. She's hungry."

So we went back to Hilda's house and with great love and affection, Hilda decided to make her a couple of sandwiches. I still remember this day as if it were yesterday. First she made her a couple of cheese sandwiches, and then she decided that she should put some lettuce on the sandwich, because she probably didn't have any green vegetables. Then she decided she needed some vitamin C, so we hunted around and found an orange. And of course we had to get her a napkin.

Hilda said, "You know, she's cold. Let's find her a blanket." So we went to the hallway and got out a bunch of blankets. I thought that the brown one would be good, but Hilda said, "You know, if Jesus were here, he would say, 'Give your coat plus your cloak,' I shouldn't give her an old blanket. I should give her my favorite blanket." So we went into Hilda's bedroom.

Hilda had a very soft, light blue blanket. It was the kind you just wanted to cuddle up in. Hilda said, "I want to give her this one. If we're going to give anything, I want to give this one."

So then, of course, the phone rang and Hilda took a couple of calls and we prayed. I remember one call that was from Colorado, a woman with cancer. We prayed. After the phone call, in the living room, Hilda noticed that the plants hadn't been watered. So we did that too. And of course as she was watering the plants, she'd talk to each one. The one in the corner that Rajah, Shanti and Valli's father, had brought in once had been real little and was growing very tall. So Hilda talked to the plant for awhile. She said, "My, you're growing big and tall. It won't be too much longer before you'll outgrow this apartment." This was the kind of rhythm that we had.

We then went to the lady. Hilda gave her the food, talked to her, and gave her the blanket. Then we went to the pizza shop on 103rd and Broadway. While we were there, a drunk came in. He was very bent over. He looked at Hilda and he started talking to her. He said, "You know I'm no good. I've ruined my life. I'm just no good." Hilda touched him on the forehead and she said, "Never say you're no good. You're a child of God." I never forgot that.

I think the thing that moved me so much, being with Hilda, was that I never saw her treat anybody differently. Whether she was talking to the doorman, to someone who delivered groceries, to a priest, to disciples, she related to everyone's soul, and she loved everyone.

Hilda accepted all paths. She accepted all religions, but as a young woman she gave herself to Jesus and it was Jesus whom she married. When we were working on the *Dear Hilda* book, Hilda wrote a talk on Jesus to be included in the book. She said to me that she felt that this talk summed up her personal spiritual relationship with Jesus. So I would just like to read a couple of paragraphs from the talk that Hilda wrote on Jesus.

> May I tell you a simple story of my Jesus, the one I know so well, the one I dearly love, who never died or rose but just is and never changes through eternity, never changes with the seasons, whether it be Christmas, Easter, summer, winter, fall or spring?

> I love him well, this Lord of mine. Perhaps, as my love story unfolds, this love so full might embarrass some of you whose heads are so full and hearts not yet simple. My heart

overflows and tears run down my face as I think of the mighty man of will Who was always depicted on a cross, head down, blood dripping still. I took my Lord off the cross and found a mighty force, enough to build edifices around the world, even in villages of India and far off lands, though he trod this Earth two thousand years ago. Jesus started to teach me deep in my heart and head. He said, "Love is the answer. Love is divine. If you cannot love your brothers, then you cannot understand my life. I will have died in vain."

In the ensuing years, until now, as I stand here old yet young, I have wiped his face in the thousands I have stood before and told of the nails mankind has driven into his flesh again and again and themselves, too. For he said, "What you do to the least of them, you do unto me." And as I wipe each face, each bleeding heart, and with gentleness remove all fear from what man calls so loosely "mankind" and I call "him," I have felt his love well up within me and burst my heart into a thousand lights, brighter than the noonday sun.

He dwells deep within my heart, whose binding strings he did release and under his guidance, I've drawn a large circle, its circumference wide, wide enough to take in all mankind, no matter what their creed, be it Muslim, Jewish, Hindu, Buddhist, Christian. All are one to him who loved mankind enough to spill his blood. All he asked of us is to love.

Jed: I had the grace and fortune to live in Hilda's home. Many a time she would say to me, "You know, when I pass, it'll be the small things that I do that you'll remember me by." In the last two weeks, I've thought a great deal about that and it's true. I remember the simple things that Hilda did, the very, very insignificant things — how she would clean the house so meticulously. She would clean a cupboard, straighten books, tear up papers, with a joy and an enthusiasm and a love that made it not insignificant, that made it as though she were doing something in the world, as though the heavens were changing with each tear of a paper. Whenever you would help her, you felt you were doing the greatest things in the world, and time seemed to stand still. She would always tell us about Saint Therese and her Little Way. To me that was how she lived her life, doing the little things that some people didn't notice.

She loved all of us equally, whether we were famous or not. She made us feel that her love was so special, that she understood us like no other. And she made us feel that God loved us like no other. Hilda's enthusiasm for life was unparalleled. She could take something that was so mundane and make it so great. The *National Enquirer* is one of my favorite papers now, and I'd never heard of it or read it before. She could take an article in the *National Enquirer* and make a whole Thursday night class on it, and people would be quoting it like the *New York Times*. Whatever she did, she put her whole self into it with devotion and love.

In the last month of her life, she read a great deal from a book on her Satguru, Nityananda.[2] She said several times, "You know, in the past I always avoided the part of his passing, but I feel somehow now I can read it and it will have no effect on me." I know now what she meant. She often read stories from this book to us in the house. One in particular was of a young boy whose parents were devoted to the Master. He awoke from a dream on the day of Nityananda's passing and he told his parents, "The Master came to me and he said that he has to go. The great sages had come to him and there is work for him on the other side that only he can do."

I know that Hilda devoted her life to us, giving us everything that she had, and it is now that the Masters of the Great White Lodge and the holy ones on the other side have work that only she can do. And she is about her Father's business now. Hilda was so much to all of us. Often she would tell us on a Thursday night of the great ones, her teachers who gave her so much in this life. All of us here, for the rest of our lives, will always be able to say, "I sat, I listened, I loved one of God's great ones, Hilda Charlton."

David: After a long night's vigil, eight of us stood in a small intensive care unit at the hospital not far from here, and on the bed that we surrounded was the body that Hilda Charlton used to teach us and to bring love through. We all stood in silence as the sound from the machine that monitored her vital life signs ended and there was only a beep. We stood in silence, each in our own world. Then within my mind, I heard her speak to me. She said, "Why is everybody so somber?" I looked and I saw a light coming into the room, and with this light came a wonderful sense of bliss. The light got stronger and stronger, stronger than any sunlight. I could hardly look into it for any length of time. Then it exploded with rays reaching out all over the Earth. I knew that this was Hilda's blessing, that these light rays were going out to all those who loved her. They were touching those who had met her, had heard her on a tape, had come to a meeting, had just heard someone talk of her. And that was confirmed so much in the next few days, as I talked to so many people. Each experienced in that moment, as so many of you have told me, a miracle.

Bliss intensified in the room and my mind could only speak, "Hilda, thank you. Hilda, thank you. Hilda, thank you. Hilda, thank you for coming into our lives. Thank you for bringing love. Thank you for goading us on and pushing us up the path, for dragging us and inspiring us. Thank you." And I felt such a freedom. I felt she was free. The last part of her life was truly a sacrifice. She wanted to be here for all of us and she gave all of herself. It was a very difficult time, and now she was free.

A little bit later, as I was walking home, I met a person who had had a grudge against me for eight years and as we talked the person said, "David, I don't know why, but I love you. I don't understand it, but I love you." That confirmed this wonderful blessing she left on the Earth. As I sat that day, letting the events of the day flow through me, a vision was sent to me. It was Hilda and she was standing with Saint Therese. They were together blessing the world. Then in a little while, another vision came, and there was Hilda again, standing with Ammal, and radiant, divine grace was flowing from them. Finally, she appeared once more and she stood with Mary. And then I understood. She was telling me that Mary hasn't left the world — she's appeared in so many places, she's appeared in China, in Yugoslavia, in Spain, in Portugal, all over the world. Ammal is always finding us parking places and finding lost keys, opening difficult situations up to us, breaking down barriers and leading us on. Saint Therese gave up her heaven world so she could be close to the Earth to be with us. And what Hilda was saying is that she too is here. Just like Saint Therese, she has stayed close to the Earth and she will be with us. Glory to you, Hilda!

Ingrid: There are two very special people so dear to Hilda's heart, always and forever, Valli and Shanti. Hilda raised them from infants and trained them in the spiritual life. We will first hear from Valli, and then Shanti will sing poetic songs that Hilda loved.

Valli: Hello. My earliest memories of Hilda are from when I was a toddler. In my mind's eye, I can see glimpses of myself in a walker, rolling down the hallway, chasing after Hilda and having Hilda and Shanti laughing hysterically. Hilda has retold this story to me many, many times. To this day, I'm unsure whether the memory is in fact hers or mine. All of those sensations and feelings of those early days are so real to me now. I can close my eyes, and Hilda, I can feel the warmth that you exuded and the calm that always surrounded you. I can even smell the sweet scent of a mix of incense and perfume that always went with you everywhere and stayed with everything you touched. These were only slightly betrayed by the strength of your hand and the lilt in your walk, which suggested and reminded us of the more forceful side of you, the one that I knew so well.

I can remember you explaining everything to me. There were the mundane things, like how to use the washing machine. And then there were the times when you would sit me down when I was crying, and you would explain to me why I was here on this planet that seems so foreign, and that some day soon I would begin to understand it more, when I reacquainted myself here. These two worlds you've bridged so well came together for me in you, in your person, body and great soul.

As I stood there, by your bedside, I found myself wondering what this planet, the one that you introduced me to, would be like without your presence. But I had to remember there was the other side, the real you, that would not disappear. I remember a story you told me of your father's passing and how all those years ago, you had nothing to comfort you because you had not yet come into understanding of this other life. I also remember how you told us that the Masters instructed you to let your own mother go and how she had released you.

It is hard for me now, Hilda, to put this into words, because you were and are everything to me. You were my mother, my teacher and yes, even my pupil, as you told me when I came home from school at five years of age, so proud when I taught you some French words I'd learned that day. I still can feel the surprise I felt when I found out you didn't know everything. But as I grew older, I came to truly understand how much you knew in comparison to me and most everyone else.

I remember walking down the street with you, holding your hand which was warm and soft. We'd take off briskly on a cold winter's morning before I began school, and your fuzzy cotton coat would rub against my cheek. I also remember those private moments when we would meditate, sometimes just you and I together, and we would go off for hours. Those other worlds, you introduced those to me also. And it's true, as I grew older we didn't always see eye to eye, but there's this part of my heart, Hilda, and there I know I cannot completely belong to anyone else the way I belong to you.

And so here I was, standing by your bedside, and I remembered the last time I saw you, just recently before you passed. You took me into your room and you sat me down on your lap, and you said, "I'm so glad I have my little girl again." I think that if I could have had my way, I would have had time stop. I would have wished that we could stay that way forever. But as usual, you had a surprise up your sleeve, and that wasn't how it was meant to be.

And so, as I leaned over to kiss you good night for the last time, as I'd done all my life, I think I came to an understanding. I had to let you go, because you were not mine and you were not ours to hold, but you were so much more. I knew that some day in the future, I would be with you again, close. Until then, I ask you, Hilda, to keep watch over me and all of us, and if you see us going a little bit wrong, just sort of nudge us back over. I just want you to know that we and I love you now and always. Thank you!

Shanti: Valli is better at words than I am, and she's managed to put into those words a lot of the feelings about Hilda that I've been feeling over the past couple of weeks. Hilda was the one who taught me to meditate. She was the one who taught me to love God. She was the one who kissed my teddy bear at night. She was the one whose bed I would jump into if I was scared. So, to avoid speaking, I decided that the best way I could express my feelings for Hilda was through singing, since that's what I usually did. I usually sang for her. I chose these songs that she has had me sing time and time again, here and at home and just forever. I sang them for her again on Christmas. So I'll sing them for you once again, Hilda.

Shanti sings.

> *It had been a tradition, at the final class of every year, that candles were distributed to each person, and, in celebration of the holidays, Hilda would take the white candle on the altar and light the candles of the people in the front of the room. In the darkened room, they in turn would light the candles of those behind them until all the candles in the room had been lit from the one flame. Then all would hold their candles high and sing. It was always an experience where one could feel the holy light of God and all present as one.*

Ingrid: In this moment, let us light our candles and hold them, brightly shining, with Hilda, our Lord Jesus and the Masters of the Great White Lodge.

Everyone sings "Silent Night"

Hilda, we raise our candles in tribute to you and offer our gratitude and thank you for all that you have given us.

> Flower in the night,
> A stand for truth and right,
> A master soul that takes my heart away,
> Perched on high above,
> Hands outstretched with love,
> Breathing forth the sacred holy breath.
>
> Lazumma, Lazumma, Lazumma, Aum
>
> So let our spirits soar,
> To touch the distant shore,
> A rainbow warrior of planet Earth.
> A new age filled with light,
> With freedom, love and right,
> Lazumma, fill my night with love.
>
> Lazumma, Lazumma, Lazumma, Aum

That evening, as everyone sang "Silent Night" and then "Lazumma," a breeze was felt going through the hall, the same breeze that had been felt when Hilda had invoked the Holy Spirit. The candle flames of those standing near the urn of her ashes were blown so intensely that those candles quickly melted.

After the singing, soft music was played as people filed past her urn. Each person was given a flower.

Notes

Chapter One

1. Hilda's first two talks of 1987 have been combined into one chapter since the material she talked about in those classes was similar.
2. cf. Revelations 6:1-2
3. Hilda is referring to once the three days of darkness are actually underway.

Chapter Two

1. Rev. 7:1-2
2. Rev. 7:3

Chapter Three

1. *Hasidic Tales of the Holocaust*, Yaffa Eliach (New York: Avon Books, 1982).
2. Ibid., "The Rain(II)" and "A Passover Melody(III)," pp. 90-93
3. Rev. 3:16

Chapter Four

1. Hilda often instructed students that if they heard a voice and wanted to make sure it was authentic, they should ask three times "In the name of Jesus Christ who are you?" She said if the voice persisted it was a true voice.
2. Lahiri was a student of Babaji's who attained enlightenment and became the guru of Sri Yukteshwar, who in turn taught Yogananda. Lahiri got an unexpected job assignment from the government in the Himalayas. Soon after he arrived, while taking a walk he met a young ascetic, who turned out to be Babaji. He took Lahiri to a cave in which Lahiri had spent much of a previous life, and Lahiri realized in a flash who he truly was. When Lahiri returned to town, he got a telegram saying the assignment had been a bureaucratic mistake and he was to return home immediately.
3. Throughout this section Hilda is paraphrasing from *Personal Recollections of Joan of Arc* (New York: Harper and Brothers Publishers, 1899), p. xi.
4. Ibid., p. xi-xiii
5. Anne Frank, *The Diary of a Young Girl* (New York: Simon & Schuster, Inc., 1958)

Chapter Five

1. Music and Lyrics by Larry Heisler.

Chapter Six

1. Hear, O Israel, the Lord our God, the Lord is One.

Chapter Seven

1. *Meditations with Hildegard of Bingen.* Trans. by Gabriele Uhlein, osf (Santa Fe: Bear & Company, Inc., 1983), p. 77.
2. Ibid., p.77.
3. The stock market took a plunge in October of 1987.

Chapter Eight

1. E.B. Duffy, *After the Change Called Death* (Flagler Beach, FL: Life Forces Research Foundation, 1987).
2. Ibid., p.2.

Chapter Nine

1. This talk was given by Hilda to the Holistic Health Association of the Princeton area in Princeton, New Jersey, on December 1, 1987.
2. When camphor is burned, it leaves no residue; hence, it is offered to symbolize the burning away of impurities in a person.

Chapter Eleven

1. Planet is equated with a plane of consciousness.

Chapter Twelve

1. The vel is the spear held by Skanda; it symbolizes the flame of Jyoti, the Divine Goddess of Light.
2. M.U. Hatengdi, *Nityananda - The Divine Presence* (Cambridge, Massachusetts: Rudra Press, 1984).

Appendix

The talks included in this book were presented on the following dates:

Chapter 1   Born Again: February 26, 1987

              Holy Spirit — Breath of God: March 26, 1987

Chapter 2   The Real You: April 30, 1987

Chapter 3   Courage and Mastery: May 28, 1987

Chapter 4   Live to Your Highest Potential: June 11, 1987

Chapter 5   Divine Hints for Spiritual Growth: June 25, 1987

Chapter 6   Imprisoned Glory Released: September 24, 1987

Chapter 7   The Power of Grace: October 29, 1987

Chapter 8   Hereafter Revealed: November 19, 1987

Chapter 9   My Story: December 1, 1987

Chapter 10   Our Goal on Earth: December 3, 1987

Chapter 11   The Last Lesson: January 28, 1988

Chapter 12   Hilda Remembered: February 14, 1988

Glossary

The definitions in this glossary are limited to the specific content of this book and do not claim to be authoritative.

Avatar — An incarnation of the Hindu God Vishnu who comes to Earth to help humankind attain freedom.

Bhagavad Gita — A portion of the Mahabharata, a Hindu epic, in which Krishna gives humanity his spiritual teachings; literally, "Song of God."

chakras — The seven spiritual energy centers or "lotuses" arrayed upward in a person from the base of the spine to the crown of the head.

Count Saint Germaine — The Master in charge of developing humanity's spiritual nature through the use of ritual and ceremony.

darshan — The blessing one receives from being in the presence of a great soul.

Hierarchy — See Masters.

ida — The cooling psychic nerve center flowing through the left nostril.

Intergalactic Council — Assembly made up of beings from throughout the universe who have converged around Planet Earth at this time to guide the human race to a peaceful future and to aid in the event of disaster.

Master Hilarion — The Master who influences the scientific world and the world of poetic writing as well as the world of sound and color.

Masters — Perfected beings who out of great love and compassion have chosen to stay close to Earth to guide and teach humanity.

Nityananda (1900?-1961) — Considered by many to be a divine incarnation, Nityananda, whose name means "eternal bliss", is widely revered throughout India for the many miracles that occurred through his love.

Nostradamus (1503-1566) — Medieval doctor of medicine who prophesied the future of humans on Earth. Many of his predictions have been borne out by time.

Padre Pio (1887-1968) — Italian Catholic monk and mystic, well-known for receiving the stigmata and for his holiness.

pingala — The heating psychic nerve current which terminates in the right nostril.

Ramakrishna (1836-1886) — An Indian Master considered by many to be a divine incarnation. Although a Hindu, he personally experienced and recognized the truth in all of the major religions.

Ramana Maharshi (1879-1950) — An illumined teacher in southern India whose ashram was at the base of Arunachala, a sacred mountain. The core of his teaching was to go deeper into the true Self by focusing on the question "Who am I?"

samadhi — The superconscious state in which a person loses all sense of self and merges with the Absolute; also, a holy person's place of burial.

Sathya Age, Age of God — The time prophesied in many religions in which a fundamental change in human consciousness will occur and humans will live in oneness, harmony and love.

Sathya Sai Baba (1926 -   ) — Considered by many to be a divine incarnation, or avatar, he teaches the paramount importance of love and service to others. His ashram is located in his birthplace, Puttaparthi, in southern India.

Shambala — The golden city, on a subtle plane of Earth, from which the Masters guide the unfoldment of Earth's divine destiny.

Saint Therese (1873-1897) — A Catholic saint whose way of simplicity and love as expressed in her autobiography *The Story of a Soul* has inspired millions; popularly known as The Little Flower.

Vivekananda (1863-1902) — Close disciple of Ramakrishna, trained by him to continue his work by spreading his message. Vivekananda's lectures in the United States led to the founding of the Vedanta Society.

Yogananda (1893-1952) — A great spiritual master from India who traveled to the United States and started the Self-Realization Fellowship in 1920; author of *Autobiography of a Yogi*.

Golden Quest Publications

The following books are available from Golden Quest:

For a complete catalog of books, write to:

Golden Quest
P.O. Box 190
Lake Hill, NY 12448

Hilda's Lessons of Life

More than 300 audio cassette tapes of classes given by Hilda Charlton from 1976 through 1988 are available. The titles include:

04/05/79	Dreams
09/24/80	Blueprint for the Golden Age
01/08/81	The Divine Child within Us All
05/12/83	Discrimination — Inner Flame
03/01/84	Involution and Evolution
05/03/84	Lost Love Found
06/14/84	Angel's Guidance
10/25/84	Ego and Ego-Breakers I
11/01/84	Reality of Angels and Space Brothers
11/08/84	God's Joyous Path
03/28/85	Steps to Mastery
07/25/85	Black Holes/Universal Consciousness
11/01/85	Preparation for Earth Changes
01/30/86	Life after Passing On

For a complete catalog, write to:

Golden Quest
P.O. Box 190
Lake Hill, NY 12448